Loved Through
The Pain

Loved Through The Pain

A JOURNEY IN THE SPIRIT

Susan Wagner Carter

Loved Through The Pain

Italics in Scripture and quotes reflect the author's added emphasis.

Details in some anecdotes and stories have been changed to protect the identities of the persons involved.

ISBN-13: 9781536828672
ISBN-10: 153682867X

Library of Congress Control Number: 2016913787
CreateSpace Independent Publishing Platform
North Charleston, South Carolina

To Will

May you always see through eyes of love

And walk in strength to answer your calling

Contents

Introduction

"let us throw off everything that hinders …And let us
run with perseverance the race marked out for us, fixing
our eyes on Jesus, the pioneer and perfecter of faith."

HEBREWS 12:1

NONE OF US EVER ACTUALLY authors the book of our life. Only Jesus Christ was able to do that. It is only the retrospective look at our lives that we can describe in writing. We can choose, however, at any moment, the path our lives will follow. That is, we have the promise, through grace and faith, of following the light of the Lord, of hope, forgiveness, acceptance, and of being cleansed before God through Christ's love. Jesus secured that promise for all of us in His birth and earthly death. The pain Jesus suffered for us on the cross reflects an eternity of love for us. Through faith, accepting the Lord's love, and being changed by that love, is the one thing that we can do that allows us to write our future.

This book began with notes and journals written over a period of years. At first, I wanted to set down my personal witness, for my son Will. What began with almost a casual sense, that I wanted Will to know of occurrences that had taken place in Africa, where he and my younger son, Christian, were born, took on a sense of increasing urgency. Simply put – I have felt called to the task of writing this book.

The time has come for me to witness to God's ever attentive care and presence along the path of grace, faith, celebration, love, agony and comfort. To answer a call to give thanks for giving me the strength to continue the journey. For holding on to me so that I would not lose faith, when there was a devastating ending in my family's lives, that we could never have imagined.

I write in humility, knowing, that in the presence of the Lord, I am smaller than a grain of sand. And yet, through the Lord, as powerful as a grain of sand that lasts through generations. Assured in the words of the Bible, that the Lord has more thoughts and love for each of us, than all of the grains of sand in the world. I have hesitated in completing this book many times in the past —in concern that I could not get myself out of the way to adequately share a deeper message. Joyfully, it became apparent that the process of writing about this personal journey also created a process for listening and seeking direction. And an opportunity also, through writing and prayer, to serve and glorify the Lord.

This is not a tell-all book. Let me assure the reader that there have been many days of recalcitrance on my part that are not described. There are many days that I have said the Lord's prayer, and been thankful for the words, 'forgive us our trespasses as we forgive others.' Knowing that I have erred, I give thanks for the grace of forgiveness granted to me by the Lord and others. The events I highlight are those in which I have become increasingly aware of the work of the Holy Spirit in my life and others' lives. In several instances, I tell of my participation in national events and give my account of untold details in which I felt the Lord's presence.

We live in a world with so much tragedy; from massive events which are almost beyond comprehension to those that strike at the heart of our souls. When a personal tragedy occurs, we go through the phases, sometimes seemingly as on a broken roller coaster ride, of shock, denial, agony, and fleeting acceptance. In some cases – a grudging acceptance of knowing that life, as we knew it, has been irrevocably changed. Sometimes the passage to healing has no real ending. The journey may continue at times with more questions than with answers. There comes the day when those around us are ready to move on. But – we are not. And certainly, never will be able or want to forget. Sometimes closure is a dirty little word with meaning for those who are not close enough to feel the void.

I believe that God's good comes to all things. I have learned that where I am injured but willing to walk on in faith, that God's light will reach through. Through grace and faith, awful moments of pain are replaced with comfort, through unconditional love. That pain can also be used for a greater good and to restore joy. It is rarely a straight path to healing. In a heartbeat, a simple reminder may bring back the heartache--which may never entirely disappear. In this journey, in the depth of agony and height of joy, for me, my Savior, has been there. I have been blessed to the bottom of my heart and soul.

> Romans 8:28: "And we know that in all things God works for the good of those who love him, who have been called according to his purpose."

My Prayer
I have knowingly journeyed in faith since the earliest days in my memory. That journey has included the belief that "Jesus loves me", confusion about the meaning of sin, lack of understanding of who Jesus is, conflict about the Bible, a deep sense of guilt, rebellion, calls to revise my thinking or to repent, calls to serve, and calls to celebrate. This book is my witness to my understanding, that while

it is a deeply personal sojourn—it is also but another of the infinite examples of the real miracle of our lives. Of the fact that the God, who created the mountains and the oceans—and the sands—-came as Savior—to be in a personal relationship for the good of all. Never to abandon us. It is about the call of the Holy Spirit to service and the responsibility to share the Lord's message of hope with others. Lastly, it is the journey to understanding, acceptance, and celebration, that through Christ, in death there is life.

This is not a how-to book with easy answers. I write this with the expectation that some may disagree with my suppositions and conclusions. Bible references that I provide reflect passages or portions of passages that have had particular meaning for me. I am not a biblical scholar or theologian. And while I have spent many hours and years seeking, and asking the Lord for guidance, to understand the basis of my beliefs about the Bible; I also acknowledge that God reveals himself at his pace, not ours. I write in prayer, that to the best of my ability, my witness is helpful to some, wherever their path may take them and that it is a worthy witness for the Lord that I love.

CHAPTER 1

An Agony Beyond Description

———

It was not an ordinary afternoon for me. Life was moving in slow motion. The date was April 19, 2000, the Wednesday before Easter. Much as most boomers will never forget where they were when President Kennedy was shot, April 19th will never be a forgotten date for my family or me.

I thought that the weeks and months before April 19th had been difficult. I had no idea that an agony beyond description was about to be thrust into the midst of the grief of losing my mother five weeks before. I had spent those five weeks sitting in my parents' family room – sorting through papers – weeping – praying—trying to figure out next steps. I was exhausted.

My mother was a smoker for many years and showed all of the breathing, respiratory and energy issues that plague a long term smoker. She was seventy-seven years old. She quit smoking in her mid-sixties. By that time the effects had already taken their toll. Despite the signs of emphysema, however, her engagement with life overrode anyone's thought that she would not be with us for many years.

Elizabeth Hemphill Ward. I was truly blessed by my mother who was a kind, intelligent, supportive and caring person. She added to our enjoyment of life by her wonderful sense of whimsy and an appreciation of humor—most especially during times of difficulty.

My younger son, Christian, and I had made a rushed move to Florida, arriving a few days after the new year, 2000. It was a move that was already in the works. However, it took on a critical aspect when my mother became suddenly ill on New Year's Eve of 2000. From mid-January until March 9th when she died, I watched with the rest of the family—as efforts to get to the bottom of my mother's infection and to treat her failed. Unfortunately, we would be left with the feeling that, at least in part, she had been failed in the care she received in her last weeks of life. Her treatment seemed a total contrast to the care my father had received a little over a year before.

My beloved father, Ted Ward, 84, died in October 1998, fourteen months before. During my father's illness – we had seen only the best care and attention to the smallest details by the doctors and nurses. We felt truly supported by everyone. We had accepted that he had died with dignity and in peace.

In my mother's case, although she was in the same location, it was as though she was in a different hospital. In addition to her acute infection, she was labeled as having COPD. With some exceptions, there seemed to be a pervasive attitude of writing her off. Adding to our anguish were a series of mistakes which we all felt led to the inevitable. A final blow came when an on-call doctor decided to put in a 'new line' and punctured her lung. She died two days later.

Weeks after my mother's death a doctor did what few have the willingness to do in light of even a remote possibility of litigation. With tears in his eyes—he had the courage to acknowledge the mistakes and to shed light on the situation. Nurses and doctors had become embroiled in a major policy fight with insurance companies and management. It had been clear that my mother's care was not the highest priority where the hospital staff was concerned.

While my mother's infection and the effects of years of smoking may have been irreversible—she was denied the respect and attention which we all deserve in our final days. I met with the administrator of the hospital and gave her a list of thirty-five mistakes made during the six weeks that my mother was hospitalized. Later, we would be assured that hers was a case which would receive attention. At the end of the day, we were told the events which occurred served as a wake-up call to doctors and nurses alike. They had lost focus and respect for their patient. Shortly after my mother's death, we received a card from the nurses who had cared for her – and believe that both the doctors and nurses took steps to repair the breakdown in the system which had severely affected my mother's care.

Little would I realize that the events which had taken place in the hospital would become almost moot in an instant.

Now, five weeks after my mother's death, I was staying at my parents' home in Orlando. I had spent the last several weeks helping my brother sort my parents' papers, and file necessary documents with social security and others. I was exhausted, but I was slowly getting myself together.

My fatigue was not only from the move across the country and the six weeks spent in the hospital with my mother. For seven years, most days and nights, my thoughts were focused on my younger son's well-being. This particular Wednesday afternoon, however, I had been in thought about the events of the previous few weeks—and not so much on my son.

Christian, 27, had been ill for almost seven years. Part of the decision to move to Florida was to give him a break from the stress of Los Angeles. While I was still trying to make my way through the grief of losing my father, and then suddenly my mother, Christian was getting his plans sorted out. He had taken a job almost immediately where he could use his skills and he was pleased with his new work surroundings. He also found an apartment that was cheerful and seemed to fit his needs perfectly. It was in a large complex with lots of young professionals in their twenties and thirties. There were pools and tennis courts—a natural way to begin to make friends. He and I had lived in the same complex in Los Angeles, to help oversee his medication—and that seemed a viable possibility in his new complex. Even now at my parents' home where I was still staying, I was close by–available but not imposing on his privacy.

Before leaving Los Angeles, Christian's doctor had given us a prescription and had told me to take my time finding a doctor who would be well qualified to see Christian on an ongoing basis. He suggested that I consult with doctors at the University of Florida and the University of Miami for recommendations. Christian's situation was complicated. As long as he was relatively stable, the doctor wanted me to find the right doctor rather than putting Christian through an assortment of physicians who did not have the experience or specialty to deal with his history. The fact that he had gotten a job and was pleased with his digs gave me a sense of security. I had started the process of talking with professionals—but did not feel a sense of urgency.

During his seven years of illness, I had 'read' Christian well. I had been able to spot when he was going into crisis. While he struggled a bit when we first arrived in Orlando, he had set up his new apartment, and was studying so that he could renew his securities license. He expressed to me that he felt so fortunate that he loved his job in Los Angeles, and now had found a job in Orlando, that he would also enjoy.

Christian's illness seemed, to begin with, grief over a failed relationship in his senior year of college. It turned out to be infinitely more significant and complicated than that. What started as extreme anxiety, progressed to obsession, suicidal ideations, paranoia, hallucinations and voices in his head. Christian had suffered through years of trying to get to the bottom of what was happening to him. He enjoyed months at a time of stability and then would sink into a crisis quickly. Each crisis came quickly to a catastrophic level. He made four serious suicide attempts in seven years. There was not a definite diagnosis, and he did not fit into the box of mental illness which would include isolation, lack of social skills, and an inability to hold a job. On the contrary, his friends often sought his counsel on issues in their lives, he had been a Westinghouse scholarship finalist, and he had both platonic and romantic long term relationships.

In the immediate family, we could see that his executive mental function levels had diminished over the years—but on that Wednesday before Easter—it seemed that we had made the right decision in moving to Florida—and that he was getting settled. My older son, Will, had moved from Los Angeles to the east coast several months before—and their father had also retired to the east coast. The move put us all on the same side of the country. I had gone over to Christian's new apartment a couple of days before that Wednesday, and he had already set up his things so that he could write and play his music, study, and relax. He said that he would come for dinner on this Wednesday evening. I was satisfied that he was holding his own.

I could not have been more wrong.

As I sat in the family room of my parents' home on that Wednesday afternoon, April 19, 2000, my parents' phone rang. A male voice identified himself as a firefighter and asked if I knew or was related to Christian. The number had been on a piece of paper in Christian's car. The firefighter explained that Christian's car was parked on the side of the road near his new apartment with the blinkers on. The car was blocking a path that the fire department needed to enter. We had shipped Christian's car from California, and a couple of times after arriving it had simply stopped running. A mechanic had not identified the particular cause. The car would stop and then start back up after the engine cooled. I told the firefighter that I believed that Christian was at work and that I would call right away. On the firefighter's request, I gave him permission to move the car. I thought that probably the car had had a problem and that Christian was either at his new apartment nearby – or at his office – a couple of miles farther from the car.

I called Christian's new employer and was referred to the manager when I asked for Christian. She said that Christian had run a couple of errands for the office in the morning and that he had returned feeling nau-seated. She said that when he returned she could see that he was ill and had sent him home. She described him as having been 'bright green' with nausea. She commented that they were happy to have him on their staff. I thanked her and started calling his cell phone. Since he didn't answer—I assumed that he was probably asleep and decided to go to the apartment to make sure he was all right. I was not overly concerned. I thought I was correct that he had had car problems and that if he was sick—he was probably asleep. I then received a second call from the firefighter asking if I had found Christian. I told him I was headed to Christian's apartment.

My brother's office was a few blocks away from the car. I called him and said I was going to Christian's and asked if it would be possible for him to make sure that Christian's car was moved. He said yes that he could do that. It was now about 3:30 P.M. and while I wanted to be sure everything was okay—I still did not feel a sense of danger.

My parents' home was only about eight minutes from Christian's new apartment. I pulled into the parking lot, and there was a black and white police car waiting for me. A young, polite police officer stepped out of his vehicle and asked if I was Christian's mother. I said yes, and he said he had been asked to meet me to ask me to go straight to the Winter Springs police station. He said he had no information other than it was about the car – and that he had been asked to meet me to give me directions. He said he had already knocked on Christian's door, and there had been no answer. I explained that Christian could be a sound sleeper and that I felt it necessary to make sure he was okay. He said that he would follow up with the manager to get a key to the apartment. He would meet me at the police station.

It was just a few minutes to the Winter Springs police department from Christian's apartment. When I went to the glass window of the lobby, a pleasant and attentive woman greeted me. She said we would be going to a conference room and asked if she could offer me a soda. I said yes and I also asked if I might use the ladies room. She waited for me outside the door and already had a drink in hand when I exited. She was chatty and verged on cheerful. She showed me into a conference room which seated twelve people comfortably. It did not appear to be an inter-rogation room. In fact, I remember thinking that it looked more like a corporate conference room than a police station, with soft lighting and modern paintings on the walls.

I kept trying Christian's cell phone every few minutes—and only gradually did I begin to feel a deeper sense of concern. The woman who had greeted me had not identified herself as a detective or police officer. She asked me about our move to Florida, Christian's job, and other casual questions. There were no windows in the conference room, but I was aware that a considerable amount of time was passing. I received a call from my brother saying that police and fire engines were blocking the road where Christian's car was located. They had not allowed him to go to the car. He said he was going to head over to the police station.

When I hung up with my brother, I told the woman sitting with me that I felt it was not a good sign that Christian had not checked in with me. I went ahead and began to explain Christian's medical history to her. Since I had been told to come to the station because of the car—I said that I had not wanted to sound unnecessary alarms but that it was unusual for Christian not to check with me if he wasn't feeling well. I said that I would call his father in West Virginia to see if he had gotten any calls from Christian. It finally dawned on me that Christian probably was in severe difficulty. There was no answer at Christian's dad's home.

Several people came into the conference room over the next period to ask me questions. The inquiries seemed commonplace to me. I thought that something was going on that had not been explained to me but that they were checking basic information. I thought to myself that, perhaps, Christian had had a car accident and had left the scene. I hoped that a sense of panic had not sent him into difficulty.

Suddenly, the door to the conference room flung open banging against the wall. A woman, with several men behind her, walked directly to me without hesitation. She quickly identified herself as a detective. There was nothing pleasant or sympathetic when she then looked me straight in the eye and said, "Mrs. Wagner, we have found a body, and we believe it is your son."

My world blew apart.

"Oh God please no. Please God no. It can't be. Please God no." I cried that phrase repeatedly. Instantly an excruciating pain went from the back of my neck through my body. That physical pain stayed with me for the next several weeks. In the meantime, I begged God – not to let it be so.

It seemed that in each hour that followed the reality surrounding Christian's death was staggering. As I slowly quieted my sobs, the police began to ask me questions, and I too began to ask questions. Nothing could have prepared me for the answer to one of my first questions, "How did Christian die?"

Chrisitian had killed himself in the fire he set. It felt once again as though I had been stabbed. All I could do it seemed was to repeat over and over, "How could he do that!!???. How could he do that!!???."

The entire night I would also return to the lament of "Oh God, please no."

The woman detective was not one to mince words. And while it seemed as though there was blow after blow—ultimately I would be eternally grateful—because there would be answers—and no room for doubt that this was Christian's act. I could not have asked more from the Winter Springs police department. Virtually immediately they called a crisis counselor and medics to the station. At the same time, they also explained that Christian's death would be treated as a homicide until it was absolutely established that he had killed himself without any assistance.

I spent the next several hours answering questions. "Who was Christian's doctor in California? What medication was he taking? When had I last seen or talked with him? Where were his father and his brother? Did he have friends in Florida? Where did he work? How had he made other suicide attempts? Had I found a doctor in Florida? What effect had my mother's death had upon him?"

We had done everything logically we could think of to limit Christian's access to guns and medications. He had overdosed previously and had slit his wrists. At one point he told me that he had started to hang himself but stopped before it was too late. Christian was considered chronically suicidal. Thus my effort to stay close to him while allowing enough latitude for him to live normally when he was not in crisis. The law in most states is clear. Unless someone is "an immediate" threat to himself or others, in the early stage of a crisis, one can only provide loving encouragement to seek medical help. And for Christian, the slide from stability to a full blown crisis was a short fuse.

The police asked if I would remain at the station while they searched Christian's apartment. They let me know, shortly after they entered, that he had left a suicide note. They would not tell me the content. They then asked if I would accompany them to the flat to see if I saw anything out of the ordinary at the apartment. Everything was in order; as though everything was perfect in Christian's life. On his music stand was a cassette. It had a label on it to me. The police listened to it with me and then let me take it with me. It was the last song that Christian wrote and recorded. I would carry that cassette with me and play it hundreds of times over the next months.

I asked the police to let me contact Christian's father and brother before they contacted them. I called his father's house and reached a baby sitter for his young children. I did not explain why I was calling but asked him to call the restaurant for which he had the number and ask Christian's father to return home. I could tell from the baby sitter's voice that he understood that this was not a good call. Once I reached Christian's father and delivered this horrific information—I asked him to drive the two hours to our older son's apartment to tell him in person what had occurred. I did not want Will to be alone or to learn by phone what had happened.

We would not get to see Christian again. The police and grief counselor strongly urged that we not attempt to see him. I quickly agreed that I did not want my last remembrance of him to be his badly burned body.

The detectives went on to say that they would have to have dental records to confirm his identity totally. His body was sent to the Volusia County Coroner's Office for an autopsy and identification. There was one area on his leg where they had identified a scar, and I confirmed that he had that scar. Because I never saw Christian again—the fact that the police were so thorough both that day and in the following weeks—kept any seed of doubt about whether that was Christian, from festering in the deep vestibules of my brain, that did not want these events to be real.

Christian Read Wagner
August 30, 1972-April 19, 2000
Playing the music he loved

CHAPTER 2

Out of the Ashes

———◆———

Thoughts of suicide fall along a continuum of loss of light
into a tunnel of darkness.

It is when the darkness takes over that suicide takes place.
The darkness may be sudden or gradual.

The likelihood is that an attempt will be followed by regret.

In most cases, regret can be the basis for hope and healing.

Tragically, for some, acting in a moment of darkness,
may mean that they never have the opportunity for regret.

SEVERAL YEARS AFTER MY SON'S death, I was asked to serve on a council, whose purpose, in part, was to intervene in situations where individuals had become suicidal or had made suicide attempts. I served on the council for six years. My thoughts below reflect not only my experience with my son but also some of the collective experience of those six years.

My purpose in writing this book is to witness to my journey of faith and hope. However, it should be read in light of full understanding that, in my eyes, suicide is never a good answer or a viable last resort for solving what seems an unresolvable situation.

It has been sixteen years since my son's death. I have reached acceptance that I did not have the answers to prevent his suicide, and I have experienced untold comfort from the Lord. But no one should misunderstand. For years, there were virtually no days that I did not feel the sting of death, loss, and sadness, during many moments of the day. Even now, sixteen years later, from time to time there might be a memory which catches me by surprise; or a day when I will think about how it felt to spend time with Christian and now feel that void.

Christian is always in my heart. I am still his mother, who along with faith, will experience the loss of my child for the rest of my life. More tragic, however, is when, after a suicide, children, and siblings, about whom a person cares most, wind up experiencing years of pain, abandonment, confusion, guilt and shame, because suicide was not prevented. A year after my beloved son's death, I sat in a support group with adult children, whose parents or siblings had committed suicide as much as twenty years before, who were still struggling to forgive themselves for unwarranted guilt or anger surrounding their loved ones' deaths. Thus the tragedy of the loss of hope is carried forward.

It is my hope that these pages will serve as a call and roadmap to hope for anyone who contemplates this tragic course or for those who have had to walk this sad path and have not sought support to deal with the tragic outcome. While I have relied relentlessly upon the Lord, I also accepted professional and community support for several years following my son's death. I do not believe that I would be married, in a healthy relationship with my older son, and an active member of my community without the assistance, effort and willingness to travel the arduous path to healing.

One of the comments, made to me within hours of my son's death, and the horrific realization of what had occurred, was by a priest, who said to me, "That's not where he is now." That statement allowed me to pull myself up, at least momentarily, to focus away from the actual occurrence. It was a true statement. Christian was no longer at that spot. He was now on a different journey. Two other people pointed out to me that in biblical, Greek and native American storytelling, there are variations of the story of a phoenix rising from the ashes to new life. There is no doubt in my mind that Christian believed he was going home to the Lord. Arising anew from the ashes. But it does not change the tragedy that he felt that this was his only way out.

The reality is, that at first thought of hurting oneself, one must INTERRUPT the idea. Do whatever needs to be done immediately to turn attention elsewhere. And it may be a small thing. One night, with Christian, I felt he was edging into troublesome territory. I suggested that we go to his favorite barbecue spot. He agreed. By the end of dinner, we were laughing and talking. He later admitted to me that he had had self-destructive thoughts on his mind when I diverted his attention.

The next step is to SEEK HELP. No matter one's faith, religion, or circumstances, when that door is inched open, a path to danger is exposed. Whether it is talking with a family member, a friend, a clergy, a counselor, a doctor or even the police, it is time to reach out. It is not safe to depend on one's self to close and lock that door. It is crucial to find a good listener and a soft heart.

It is my belief that there is no such thing as a false suicide attempt. Or merely a cry for attention. Because someone fails to take deathly action, an attempt, or a momentary declaration, should never be minimized. Such a moment, no matter the scenario means that the person has dangerously lost the connection with those around him, however briefly, to sustain life.

John 10:10 "The thief comes only to steal and kill and destroy; I came that they may have life, and have it abundantly. "

Simply said, there is never a moment that the Lord wishes us to steal and kill and destroy. The Lord came that we might have life. While the Lord may forgive our actions — it should never be perceived or confused that the Lord wishes any one of us to destroy the beautiful life God has created in us.

During our lives, virtually all of us experience, at some moment, or perhaps, sadly, even for years, guilt, shame, embarrassment, rage, grief, pain, agony, and at times, loss of hope.

When we experience guilt, it is a sign that we have missed the mark in our lives. It is the notice that we need to stop, look and listen. It is the yellow light at an intersection of our lives.

When we experience shame, it is a red light. It may be that we have cut off our connection to God's presence by repeatedly turning our backs on what we know is right. That we have taken our guilt to the point that we no longer see the possibility of the Lord's love and forgiveness, or that we have accepted someone else's evil declaration of our lack of value. It is, in shame, that we are called, at the deepest levels of our souls, to seek light. It is through courage, not suicide, and the willingness to travel the necessary journey, to a place of hope and healing, that the Lord wants for all of us.

When we experience embarrassment, we may lose ourselves and put ourselves at the mercy of others. We make ourselves the center of focus that may exaggerate our importance in others thoughts or intensify the significance of the occurrence. Having said that, no one should under-estimate the pain that we can cause others through meanness, bullying or false humor.

If our embarrassment is a result of our silliness or momentary bad judgment, once again, it should serve only as an indicator that a change of direction is necessary. Never as a source for self-condemnation. I have several lifetime memories of embarrassment. Some I can laugh at now. In one case, as an adult, a school hood friend sought my forgiveness for her actions against me in junior high school. We have lessons we learn from those times. May they never come at the cost of life.

When we experience rage—retribution is never the answer. It is in rage that we are at greatest risk of destroying, in an instant, all that would ever have meaning for us. I have talked with suicidal individuals who, once they were able to get help, expressed that there was a moment when they thought only of the lesson that they would 'teach' someone else; a lesson followed by the realization that they might have created untold destruction if they had acted on their thoughts.

Destruction as an answer is a lie. It is evil. It creates irreparable destruction.

Thoughts of destruction CALL FOR ALARMS at every level to be sounded. There will never be regret by an individual who, in a moment of rage, responds to the tiniest thought of seeking help, by turning to others for help, rather than destruction, to work their way out of their dark place.

Again, the moment that we know of someone who has inched the door open to thoughts of suicide, we cannot overestimate the importance of getting professional help and providing support. Tough love, I believe, is never the answer to such a situation.

The journey that my son faced was a seven-year history of illness and pain. He was in a small percentile who become chronically suicidal because of physical illness. He knew that something terrible was happening to him. Slowly the light dimmed.

Christian sought help. He participated in treatment. He slowly gave up hope that he would heal. Always, for me, there was the hope that we would find an answer around the next corner. Some of those answers have come since his death. I do not allow myself to go down the path of 'what if'.

I hope that anyone experiencing a period of desolation will ask himself or herself the question, what if, I get help. After each attempt that Christian made to kill himself, and after each hospitalization when we reached him as he went into crisis, he expressed that he was grateful that he had survived. Once out of the crisis, he had the desire to live.

For more than 99 percent of people who contemplate suicide there is help to be found and hope for a healed life. Having said that, there is a suicide, in the United States, approximately every thirteen minutes of the day. We must do better as a nation to reach those who lose hope.

CHAPTER 3
Total Dependence

———

For seven years I felt as though God had answered my prayers to keep Christian alive. From the beginning, I had recognized that I could do all in my power to try to support and help him but that I was not in charge. I had spent hours researching his symptoms, looking for doctors who could help him. All of the family adored him. He was a spectacular young man who had brought years of joy into our lives.

Our love for him was unconditional and totally deserved. Christian knew something terrible was happening to him. And it was agony for him at times. Repeatedly, he had looked at me and pleaded for me to tell him why this was happening to him. There was little I could say to him to explain what was taking place. Always, to maintain our closeness, I had to be honest with him that I did not have answers.

Christian's doctors were among the finest in the country. They could not explicitly identify the unraveling that was occurring. Their months of encouragement not to give up – turned into years. Each year brought hope that research would yield a solution. Each period of stability brought the hope that the worst was behind him. And each recurrence became more devastating.

The doctor in California felt a move to Florida, with less stress and family, would be positive. Christian said he wanted to make the move.

The proposed move, of course, did not anticipate my mother's sudden illness. Christian seemed to cope with his grandmother's unanticipated death.

His efforts to get a job and to find an apartment appeared to confirm that we had made a positive move. He had told both his doctor and me, some months before, that he did not believe he would make another suicide attempt. We both knew that whether he went into crisis depended on his physical status. In the past, he had articulated that he still considered suicide a possibility. So his disclaimer was a positive sign.

All of the family and his friends maintained a close relationship with Christian throughout. Doctors had told him repeatedly that it was critical that he maintain virtually daily contact with me, because repeatedly, I noticed subtle changes which were indicators of an imminent downward slide. If I did not see him for a day—I certainly had a conversation with him.

The element that changed, aside from our move, was his medication. Christian only responded to medications for a period of months. The drugs that he was prescribed treated symptoms—and were not curative. A new drug was coming on the market, Zyprexa. It was touted as having a healing aspect. We had reached the end of the line on other medication and sought permission from the FDA to allow Christian to receive the medication before it's formal release.

At first, it seemed to be what we hoped. He stabilized, and there were fewer side effects than the other medications that he had taken. One medication required weekly blood tests. On another, he slept fourteen or fifteen hours a day. And for a period the extra hours of sleep were a welcome relief. For the first time in months I could sleep without having to stay vigilant for nighttime movements. It was later my conclusion – along with his doctors – that the new medication had once again temporarily treated the symptoms – but in this instance also masked a loss of effectiveness.

Only after Christian's death would doctors reach a tentative conclusion which seemed to answer the question as to what had happened to this amazing young man. Christian's father was a US State Department officer and we served in embassies in Africa, for six years. As a baby, Christian became ill, and we were evacuated to the American Hospital, in Paris, for a month. At that time, he was diagnosed with both a bacterial infection and an acute viral infection. Following that episode, Christian was in good health. There were no other unusual health occurrences during his childhood. However, in high school, there seemed to be a recurrence of virtually the same symptoms he had suffered as a baby. Once again he was diagnosed as having an acute virus. This fact would become a key factor in the minds of the doctors.

Every single doctor who dealt with Christian during his illness made extraordinary efforts to find both the causes and solutions for what was taking place. Several times doctors removed themselves – as Christian was considered chronically suicidal – and they felt they could not find a solution.

On two occasions, doctors sat with me and wept. They saw Christian as an extraordinary person – and felt the deep pain and frustration that he would stabilize only temporarily.

Over time Christian appeared to be losing some of his reasoning capabilities as well. At that point, doctors felt it necessary to remind me repeatedly that no matter our efforts, that there was a better than sixty percent chance that out of the blue—without warning—Christian might kill himself.

We had no guns, kept knives out of sight, and accounted for any medication in the house. In other instances, I had realized that he was 'sliding' quickly, and we had reached him. Doctors considered it a miracle that he had survived a couple of his tries. I credited God that I had the instinct to realize when something was happening and reached him. I never, ever, for one moment considered that his death was inevitable. I relied upon Psalm 121 both before and after his death.

Psalm 121:1-8 "I lift up my eyes to the mountains—where does my help come from?

My help comes from the Lord, the Maker of heaven and earth.

He will not let your foot slip—he who watches over you will not slumber; indeed, he who watches over Israel will neither slumber nor sleep.

The Lord watches over you—the Lord is your shade at your right hand; the sun will not harm you by day nor the moon by night.

The Lord will keep you from all harm—he will watch over your life; the Lord will watch over your coming and going both now and forevermore."

Eventually, I would accept that for Christian, in death, there was life. He is safe. I had at times worried about what would happen to Christian in the future. I thanked the Lord many times that Christian chose to stay close to me. I prayed daily that Christian would be healed, and I believe the Lord kept that promise. I believe in the safety of the Lord's hands Christian has been healed.

Following Christian's death, doctors would give a final diagnosis, a reflection of years of research, that they believed Christian had contracted a retro virus as a baby, which intertwined and slowly destroyed the DNA of his brain. They finally were able to provide research to me on the devastating effect on the brain of this virus. Today, researchers believe it is the same virus which causes multiple sclerosis.

The complexity of mental illness and the lack of both medical and general public understanding remains a sad reality. The interpretation of the Baker Act (the law in most states that allows a hospital hold to be placed on an individual) remains subject to huge variations with sometimes lethal results. The law reflects a concern for the rights of individuals to hold their personal beliefs without fear of incarceration, mixed with litigation resulting from false holds. It further reflects the difficulty in pinpointing the moment that an individual will slide into irreversible crisis. Only through the coordinated efforts of professionals, technology, families, communities, and research – meaning resources – can true hope be realized. Despite what is now a national dialog, there is a vast distance to be traveled in so many states that have substituted jail cells for medical care. As a society, may we bring both the Lord's love and the best in combined resources to enable families and communities to achieve hope for those who suffer from illnesses which affect the brain.

Going back to that police conference room in Winter Springs, I have described to people that at the moment the detective spoke to me—aside from the physical pain that I felt—and my cries and pleas that it was not Christian in that fire, I felt as though God's hands had gone around me. I felt God saying to me,

"I have hold of you, and I won't let go!"

In the minutes, days and months following Christian's death—I was entirely dependent upon God's love, steady hand, comfort, care and grace to make it through. In the midst of this indescribable agony, the rest of my family and the world also put their arms around us. I cannot help but be so grateful and thankful for the care that everyone gave. That care could not reach to the core, however, to deal with the agony of losing our beloved Christian. Only the Lord could do that.

CHAPTER 4

Starting at the Beginning

———◆———

"Jesus loves me! This I know,
For the Bible tells me so;

Yes, Jesus loves me!
Yes, Jesus loves me!
Yes, Jesus loves me!
The Bible tells me so."

THIS SONG I REMEMBER FROM my youngest days. I not only learned the words—I felt the meaning as well. I grew up in a family with a lot of laughter along with a fair share of pain. I seemed to have almost an innate sense that as a little child – my antics brought joy to others. Fortunately, virtually all of the children in my family had that same sense. In other words, because we had loving parents, grandparents, and aunts and uncles who fostered a sense of joy in our lives—we were able to bring joy to others as well. I have heard people say that children view God by the way they are treated by their parents. We were blessed by parents who let us know that we brought them joy – and by extension felt the same was true for God.

Coming into real communion with the Lord, by the grace of God, I firmly believe, can take place at any time, under any circumstance and at any age. For each of us, it is a personal journey, each with a different time and moment that we are able, by faith, to fully accept the Lord's love. Unfortunately, there are too many children who experience unimaginable pain before they know the reality of the Lord's love.

I was baptized as a baby in the Episcopal church, attended Sunday school, was confirmed at twelve, attended youth group in junior high and high school and have been an active member of the church throughout my life. That is the simple explanation of history. It does not begin to explain the journey, the Lord's saving grace or the blessing of living in the fullness of God.

I am grateful that I was in a family, that despite reservations about the church at times, provided a foundation that I could identify with through-out my life. The process of learning about the Bible, the liturgy of the Episcopal Church and the meaning behind communion would be lifelong. Along the way, there would be periods of confusion. However, like a house which stands after being whipped about in a hurricane, the blessing of a foundation, has not crumbled through times of pain, confusion, and even rebellion; and when it has been necessary for me to rebuild my life.

While some people view repetitive rituals in the church with superfi-cial understanding—or believe the participants are merely going through a rote process—for most participants—the rituals serve as a lifelong pro-cess with ever-deepening meaning. Through the liturgy and the lection-ary (Episcopal Church calendar) all individuals are invited to join others in prayer worldwide—wherever they are located.

As I traveled and lived in many locations throughout the world, I would always be grateful that I had a church home in which I could participate. At one point I would live in Guinea, Africa, where I would have endan-gered the lives of others if I attempted to attend church. While I could not be in a local church, I could turn to the litany of prayer on my own and know that I was still joining others in the worldwide church. During that period, in my mid-twenties, the Bible, prayer and meditation became the cornerstone of coping with my daily life – as well as the catalyst for a determination that I would live in total faith in the Lord.

While the Episcopal church is my home, I have engaged in a life-long search for understanding multiple denominations and religions. My maternal great grandparents were Jewish and migrated from Russia to the US, before the Russian Revolution. My grandmother attended an Episcopal High in Charleston, So. Carolina, and became a Christian in her early teens. My great grandparents respected her choice.

One of my greatest challenges in my journey, personally, has been to try to comprehend the division among Christians in the way that they relate to the Bible. There would be a day when there would be a total disconnect between my understanding and experience of a loving and caring Lord and messages from others of an angry and judgmental God.

A psychologist said to me once that neither psychologists nor theologians know why some children find a safe place in their psyche, or an early awareness of God, and others don't. I have come to believe that during a period in which I was in danger as a baby and at critical points in my childhood, that through the Holy Spirit, God made his presence known to me. And that because of the gift of viewing the world through the eyes of love that I was able to walk in faith early in my life.

While at all ages the Lord reaches out, a combination of circumstances and our own independence or stubbornness may block our ability to understand His gift of grace. Or even to know when we have received His grace. And yet, at any given moment in time, we can turn to the Lord and ask for His presence and answers.

Mathew 7:7 "Ask, and it will be given to you; seek, and you will find; knock, and it will be opened to you."

My first memories of prayer go back to about age four. Aside from prayers in Sunday school and learning the Lord's prayer, we often heard prayers for the well-being of friends and family. Then my sister, Nancy, contracted rheumatic fever and was hospitalized for extended periods. My parents would make daily trips to the hospital. Sometimes I would be at home with a babysitter—sometimes sitting in the waiting room of Variety Children's Hospital, in Miami, and sometimes sitting with one parent while the other went to spend time with my sister. During one period when I was well aware of my folks' fears regarding my sister—I specifically prayed for her safety. A diary, which I started at age six, reads – "Dear God, Please keep Nancy safe."

I, too, would be hospitalized that year and understood the difference it makes to have caring parents who provide the reassurance of safety. In the hospital bed next to me was a little girl who had only an occasional visitor. I am not sure that her parents were the ones who visited her. We were both in cribs to keep us from falling out of bed. She would reach through the slats to hold my hand and my parents would pay attention to her each time they were in the room with me. I noticed that her lips became blue and that her toes became blue as well.

In a matter of a week or so, she was transferred out of the room, and I knew that she had died the day she was moved. Later that day, my doctor, Dr. Benjamin Shepherd, would find me weeping and came to sit with me. I told him that I knew that she had died. He asked me if I was frightened that the same thing would happen to me. I answered, "No, I know God is keeping me safe. My toes have not turned blue." That would be an expression that I have said to myself throughout my life. "I know that God is keeping me safe. My toes have not turned blue". Dr. Shepherd read to me and stayed until I settled down a bit. I told Dr. Shepherd that I felt sad that my little roommate was alone when she died. And I remember a nurse saying to me, "It's okay honey. She wasn't alone. She was with Jesus."

While my sister and I went to church most Sundays—with the Deacon's family—our parents were not regular church goers. Each of my parents had had experiences in the church which made them uncomfortable. It was not particularly in defiance that they failed to attend. It seemed that because of the pressures on their marriage that church became an increasingly difficult place for them. They were present only intermittently although they stayed in close touch with the Rector of the church. While my mother had grown up in the Episcopal Church – my father had grown up with a strict Southern Baptist mother. Her efforts to control her four boys after the death of their father backfired to some degree. They wanted no part of the restrictions that she sometimes imposed. They were living through the days of the Great Depression on the tough streets of Atlanta. Not a place for the faint of heart. Or life without an occasional beer, dancing or female companionship.

At age ten I asked my father to promise that he would be confirmed with me in the Episcopal Church. He kept his word and on that day acknowledged the Lord as his savior. In the year before his death, we had conversations which indicated that he was at peace with life and ready to meet the Lord. He commented to all of us that he would 'be riding off into the sunset before long.' We would pray together in the last few hours of his life, and it was a great comfort that he was at peace.

My maternal grandmother was probably our most significant influence in prayer and church. She faithfully loved the Lord and prayed with us on every subject in life until her death at age 94. Having said that—my sister and I were often on our own in Sunday school. My grandmother attended an Episcopal Church that was far enough away that it was not practical for my sister and me to accompany her.

Occasionally being sent off to church by ourselves would cause a problem. My dear sister, Nancy Loving, is four years older than me. I have learned a great deal from her throughout my life—including in my spiritual journey. However, as small children, our Sunday school would attend the 'big church' and we occasionally found ourselves sitting next to each other. We would get the giggles, and do everything in our power not to embarrass ourselves, when someone would stumble on a word or some event would strike us as hilariously funny.

As a child, on one occasion I found myself in hot water, in the big church. It was announced that we would be singing "We Three Kings of Orient Are". I was thrilled because I knew the words by heart and as the music began, I sang out at the top of my lungs, the version my sister had taught me, "We three Kings of Orient are... tried to smoke a rubber cigar... It was loaded and exploded....." By that time the adults three rows around me had turned to give me stern looks. I realized I was singing the wrong words. Hopefully, my red face told them I had not known what I was doing. I later determined that I would only attend churches where the congregation would understand if a child made a mistake during a service. That served me well for my children. As adults, my sister and I find we still succumb to the occasional giggles when we attend church together. My brother-in-law, the Reverend John Loving, is a deeply faithful retired Episcopal priest. On occasion, he has given us the 'look' when he could see we were reverting to our Sunday school days in the big church.

Throughout my early childhood, the messages to me concerning the Lord were consistent. As my father put it, I could be an 'imp' on occasion and would be corrected. If I did something which was a threat to my safety—I would get an occasional hand to the seat of my pants to let me know that what I had done was dangerous—like running towards the street to retrieve a ball. However, the messages to me were clear—that my parents loved me, the Lord loved me and that we were a family that wanted to please the Lord. We cared about each other and others. I never once heard the word Satan as a small child. I never once heard that I should have shame – or that I was rebellious or was anything other than 'a little child pleasing to the Lord.'

> **Psalm 8 1:2 "Lord, our Lord, how majestic is your name in all the earth! You have set your glory in the heavens. Through the praise of children and infants you have established a stronghold against your enemies."**

I still have my childhood diary, always addressed to God or Our Father in Heaven – which was a five-year diary—through elementary school. It reflects my fears for my parents' safety at one point, my little girl frustration with my older sister, my goals for school work and the fact that each day—I felt I could bring the smallest problem to God. At one point, a minister said to me that as I matured, I would not talk to the Lord in that way. I would come to realize that it is for our joint good that our prayers are answered. We are called to change for the Lord, rather than asking the Lord to change for us. I also so know to this day, that I can still take either the smallest or the largest problem to the Lord.

> **Mathew 19:14 "Jesus said, 'Let the little children come to me, and do not hinder them, for the kingdom of heaven belongs to such as these."**

I wish that all children might learn that the Lord came quietly as a baby to be loved. I give thanks that it was first in safety that I learned to trust the Lord. It was through love that I came to have a better understanding of the words of how we may be changed in faith.

> **Colossians 1:9-10 "We continually ask God to fill you with the knowledge of his will through all the wisdom and understanding that the Spirit gives, so that you may live a life**

worthy of the Lord and please him in every way: bearing fruit in every good work, growing in the knowledge of God, being strengthened with all power according to his glorious might so that you may have great endurance and patience, and giving joyful thanks to the Father..."

CHAPTER 5

A Child's World is Not Always Safe

———

A FIRST LOOK AT EVIL. A series of events broke through my sphere of safety as a child. First, at about age six, a few miles from our home, a small girl was kidnapped from her grandparents' couch and brutally tortured and killed. The police were out in droves, and my best friend's mother talked to us virtually continuously about what had happened. The small girl's murderer was never caught, and I began to develop nightmares and a fear of the dark—as the descriptions made the news hourly and fear ruled the neighborhood pervasively. At one point my little friend and I became almost hysterical as a car slowed while we were walking from her house to mine. My parents tried to console us – and my mother asked my friend's mother to stop discussing it with us. But a monster had become real in my mind and left me fearful for a long time to come.

The conversations I had with my mother during this period about what to do if there was danger -- I believe saved my life a few years later. In the meantime, tragedy gripped the family of the small girl who was kidnapped—and the shield of safety that parents had reason to believe existed for their children in our neighborhood was lost. Many years later, well into our fifties, I would have a conversation with my best friend, and she too had never forgotten the fear and loss of innocence which had occurred in our small lives during that period.

I would also come to understand another form of evil at a young age. It affected me immediately and would stay with me through my life. It would be a lesson, ultimately, that I was glad I had learned at a young age. The event had the opposite effect than had been intended. At the time of my sister's illness—a person who was key to our family—was our babysitter and housekeeper—Molly. My mother was in her late twenties as she and my father struggled with the diagnosis that my sister had rheumatic fever. Molly often stayed with me while my parents went to the hospital. I often heard her giving words of encouragement to my mother. Molly was a quintessential kind, strong, and smart black woman. I felt only safety and kindness in her presence. I am sure she conveyed that same sense of safety to both of my parents. She was truly loved by my family and by me.

We lived in a neighborhood where many of our friends had swimming pools. Throughout my childhood, my parents struggled financially—compounded by medical bills and other costs for my sister and me. However, we enjoyed the benefits of neighbors with pools during the summer and would make the rounds from one pool to another.

During a period when my sister was hospitalized—Molly spent lots of time with me. She would bring her granddaughter, Mattie, with her to our home on occasion. We played well together, and I never hesitated to take her with me, when I was invited to my best friend's house for a swim.

One day after a group of us swam for a while at my friend Carol's house – our little group decided to move on to another friend's house a couple of blocks away. We would continue our fun and games at Priscilla's swimming pool. It was a morning which started out with lots of fun and laughter. After a while, though, we grew bored and moved our little party inside.

We were sitting on the beds, when the door sprang open, and Priscilla's mother flew into the room. I will never forget her angry eyes. She grabbed me by the shoulders and began to shake me hard. "How dare you!!" she yelled. She continued to shake my shoulders as she screamed, "You don't bring a nigger to my house!! Get out of here!!" The year was 1951. We could not have run faster.

I was six years old. There was no misunderstanding on my part of the hatred that she wished to convey. Or the depth of the hatred which lay behind the word nigger.

There is no innocence in that word. Anyone who denies it's significance or tries to pass off such a reference today as merely being politically incorrect—denies history. It is meant to be an expression of hatred. It is intended to hurt. And it rejects God's love of all people. Those who would deny it's meaning live a lie.

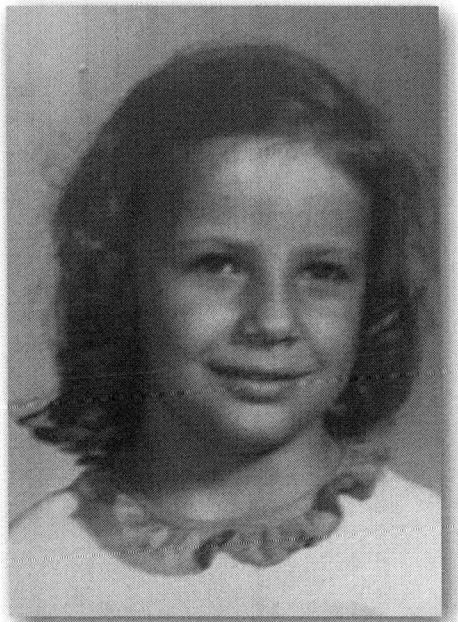

Susan at 6 years old.

At that moment I understood the ugliness of hatred. This beautiful child – who came in innocence to my home to play – was the subject of hatred. Nothing could have been more evil. Again, I was only six years old. I understood completely. There can be no misunderstanding on the part of an adult about the significance --- no matter the tone of the delivery—of the message contained in that word.

In the years that followed, as integration began to take place in the south, I would come to realize as well that some people—who supposedly were good Christians—twisted the words of the Bible to foster segregation and hatred. How important it is to listen carefully and to understand the words and meaning of those in positions of leadership both inside and outside of the church. By the same token, I also learned that where there is truly the Lord's love there can be understanding and reconciliation. Therein lies the hope that God's will – will be done on earth as it is in heaven.

Mathew 29:36 "Love your neighbor as yourself."

Word soon spread in our neighborhood of the occurrence which took place that day in 1951. My parents, of course, were outraged at this turn of events. My memory is that the parents of the other girls were equally outraged. They did not condone this woman's actions. It was her daughter who was isolated from future play in the neighborhood. I did not see much of her until high school. I then remember looking into the face of sadness. Instinctively, I knew that she had suffered from a mother who had hatred as her god. How sad for all involved.

The 1950s were the time of post-war American pie for some. Women came out of the factories, we all watched Ozzie and Harriet, and my parents, like most middle-class Americans, sought the great American dream of home ownership and good schools for their children. Our neighborhood could have been on the front cover of the Saturday Evening Post.

The houses sat on an acre of property, most of the homes had swimming pools, the wives all belonged to the Women's Club and the husbands worked hard to bring home paychecks which would keep the dream going. I would realize as an adult, however, how much 'truth' at times can be obscured. The truth was that we had a murderer, a child molester, a wife beater, and as I described above, at least one all out racist—all living within steps of our front door. Picture perfect was anything but.......

Few women during that period asked for power—and behind the mask of distinction and stature in white neighborhoods--all too often there was pain and suffering which had no vent until a tragedy occurred. We left home one morning with my parents to visit our aunt – only to return later in the day to our cordoned off street with police cars everywhere. Our next door neighbor had come home early from a hunting trip to find his wife in bed with another man. He shot and killed them both. The couple had a long history of domestic violence. However, he served less than ten years in prison for killing two people. It was the mid-1950's and wives were looked upon by the courts as chattel. There would even be the discussion among some that she had 'gotten what she deserved'.

I would soon come to learn at all too early an age that the mask of evil comes in many forms with piercing impact on a child's soul.

CHAPTER 6

What Did I Do Wrong?

———

THE EVENING STARTED OUT AS a treat. My father's business partner had come to Pompano Beach from South Miami, for his regular meeting with my dad and to go out for dinner with the family. The partner was a hero where our family was concerned. A neighbor for many years, Mr. McGlean had helped my father realize his lifelong dream of owning a small town newspaper by investing and becoming the publisher of the Pompano Beach Town News. At age 52, Mr. McGlean seemed like the quintessential grandfather. A person in whom the community had total trust. And a hero to our family because he helped my father realize his dream.

My dad had delivered his first newspaper in Atlanta when he was about eight years old. Newspapers intrigued him from the earliest age. He was one of four boys – whose father had died before he was ten. His delivery job was more than just a way to earn a little money for recreation. All of the boys worked to help support the household in the midst of the Depression.

At about age twelve, my father found he had a mentor in an English teacher. She liked his writing style and encouraged him to develop his writing capabilities. There was never any doubt about what he wanted to do. After a wrestling scholarship to Emory, he began his newspaper writing career as a sports writer for the Miami Herald. Writing was in his blood.

For a period, it looked as though my father might have to leave the newspaper business. On his salary, it was hard to pay the mounting medical bills. He pursued avenues from public relations to sales positions. It soon became apparent that he despised those jobs. He wanted to write. And after several years it seemed he found the perfect opportunity. The Pompano Beach Town News was for sale. There was great cause for celebration when Mr. McGlean became the publisher, and my father became the Editor in Chief.

I was too young to know the actual negotiations which took place. But we soon found ourselves living in Pompano Beach. I started in junior high school, and my sister started in high school.

My father had a plan for the things he wanted to do to bring the sleepy little newspaper to life. He was soon all over town – reporting on events – highlighting the high school sports teams – involving people from the community at many levels.

I found myself at a junior high school that treated newcomers as though they were old friends. We had moved several times locally during the previous years, mainly for financial reasons – and it was nice to start junior high school with all the students new to their first year as well.

I had known my father's new business partner most of my life. He and his wife had always been kind to our family. During the summer months, we would take advantage of their open invitation to use their swimming pool anytime. They often went away for the summer, and we were happy to have free access to their pool.

When we made the move to Pompano, Mr. McGlean repeatedly offered to let me return to South Miami, with him and his wife, so that I could visit my best friend, Carol, in our old neighborhood. At twelve, spending a night away from home was not a big deal, and I thought the idea of going back to the neighborhood to see Carol, was a good idea.

After several months of occasional discussion, a date was set. Per their usual weekly schedule, Mr. McGlean came to Pompano, for his meeting with my father, and then we all went to dinner. Mr. McGlean did not have his wife with him, but she would be waiting at their home when we arrived. I would spend the night at their house, go to see Carol, several doors away, in the morning, and my mother would come to pick me up in the afternoon.

Nothing seemed unusual – but before we started to leave – I suddenly had second thoughts. I made a comment to my mother about not having done my homework. She pointed out that I would be home the next afternoon. The adults were talking as I stood by the car and I found myself having a strong urge to call the whole thing off. That feeling increased in seconds to a sense of danger and something being terribly wrong. I, at that point, however, had no reason to change what had been set up and didn't know what to do – other than to get into the car.

That was a choice I would regret. I firmly believe that I was warned that I was in danger. In future years, I would pay attention to that feeling of warning and listen to that inner voice. I would come to believe that is God's voice, trying to protect me. It would serve me well in the future to pay attention to that still small voice – no matter what the outer circumstances seemed to say.

On this evening, however, I was too young to explain my feelings of fear. This person, whom my parents trusted, a pillar of the community, in a position of respected authority—would soon have me out on a dark road, twenty miles from home – molesting me. His sudden tyranny would continue again during the night with his wife in the next room. For sleeping, I was put in a room with no locks on the door. Leaving the light on in the room did not ward off this deviant. On the dirt road, I heard my mother's voice in my head, telling me if I was ever in this kind of situation – not to cause panic. In this terrifying situation – I remembered the little girl so brutally murdered in our neighborhood – and instinctively knew that I had to be still.

By the following morning, I was in a fog. I was totally confused by what had taken place and had no idea of what I should do. Mr. McGlean acted as though nothing unusual had happened. His wife made an apple pie, and I went to Carol's house. I made only brief mention to her, and she had an equally confused reaction.

Early in the afternoon my mother and my aunt came to pick me up. I sat in the backseat of the car – again still feeling in a fog and confused. After a brief exchange about whether I had had a good visit – my mother and aunt were soon engaged in conversation with little focus on me. I did not speak up and say anything.

Over the next few days I found myself asking many questions. Why did that happen? What made him think he could do that? Should I tell my parents? Did he know that what he had done was wrong? Did he believe it was ok? What did it mean that this person we all trusted did this? I had no answers.

Several days later my mother would say to me that she wanted to talk with me. She sat me down and asked if anything unusual had happened while I was visiting with Mr. McGlean and his wife. He had come back to Pompano, and my father felt he was acting in a strange manner. My father asked my mother to talk with me. I, at that point, told her what had happened.

She was crushed. Her immediate concern was to try to give me reassurance. However, she also immediately expressed that when she told my father, he might lose it and use his years in the boxing and wrestling ring on this vile person. Within minutes of talking with me, she had contacted the minister of our church and requested that he be present while she spoke with my father. In the following days, it seemed as though the whole family's world caved in. Many many questions and much chaos and confusion followed.

That chaos and confusion would continue for years. Ultimately, I would be repeating the events to the Miami district attorney. There would be months of questions. A trial. Re-victimization. My father would lose the newspaper, and there would be huge financial loss and stress between my mom and dad.

It would not go past me that if I had kept my mouth shut that perhaps the family would not have suffered so much. Years later other members of my family would admit that they had had those same feelings where I was concerned.

I began to believe that if my family was suffering so much that I must have done something wrong. God had tried to warn me. Why had this happened? Why had this man believed he could do this to me? No answers would come for many years.

In the meantime, my childhood belief and feeling that God took great pleasure in my joy for life left me wondering whether I had done something to upset God and to cause these problems. Some would say, Satan was at work. On the one hand, I would continue to participate in church activities, and it would be a home for me. But it would be some years before I would find answers to at least some of my questions. The turmoil would also continue for my whole family.

CHAPTER 7
The Little Warrior

———◆———

"I can do all things through Christ who strengthens me."

PHILIPPIANS 4:13

I AM ONE OF THE fortunate survivors of child molestation. I say that because first and foremost my parents believed me. Second, family and our
lifelong pediatrician supported me. Third, I had an incredible opportunity as an adult to come to terms with the events, questions, re-victimization
and turmoil which came to pass because I wanted to see my best friend.

Initially, my parents turned to our beloved doctor, Dr. Benjamin
Shepherd, for guidance. Dr. Shepherd had seen my sister through rheumatic fever, sat and read to me for hours, at Variety Children's Hospital,
when the little girl next to me died, and for many years past the usual age
for seeing a pediatrician, remained a friend to all of us.

On the evening after I explained to my mother what had happened – we
made a trip to Miami to see Dr. Shepherd. My parents talked with him
alone. Then Dr. Shepherd asked to see me alone. He asked me to describe
to him what had happened. My parents wanted to confirm that I had not
been raped. They then began to discuss with me the steps they felt should
take place.

Dr. Shepherd would contact Mr. McGlean and give him the opportunity to consider counseling. If he chose to deny what had taken place, with my agreement, the district attorney would be contacted. Dr. Shepherd presented to me that it was up to me – but that he hoped that I would help make sure that this man would never hurt another child.

All of the adults around me had talked to me at this point – and all expressed their feelings that this was a sick individual who needed to be stopped. I felt brave that I was about to stand up to this person.

I was present when Dr. Shepherd made the call to Mr. McGlean. It was clear at the beginning of the conversation that he had no interest in acknowledging in any way that he had molested me. Dr. Shepherd contacted the district attorney right away.

Like the Lone Ranger riding in on his great white horse – I believed that I would save others from going through this frightening and confusing experience. Soon I was making repeated trips to the district Attorney's office to repeat what had taken place. Only a small piece appeared in the Miami Herald that our former neighbor had been charged with assault and battery. My name was protected.

Soon it would begin to feel as though I was leading a double life. That of a supposedly carefree twelve or thirteen-year-old participating in school events and social activities. And that of a victim caught in a morass of questions by adults, requirements to be on my best behavior, and finally the need to keep a deep dark secret. The adults in my life feared that my name would become public and that some would think poorly of me. One day I would understand that some secrets serve to create a self-dialog of shame.

The day came when I was to go to court. By this time nothing was a laughing matter. My father had given up the newspaper and was having difficulty finding a job -- let alone a real opportunity. He was angry that he could not get immediate justice for the assault against me. He was frustrated, and things were dismal financially. It was a year later, and I was thirteen. I had matured from the small child on a dark lonesome road twenty miles from home to a teenager who had the physical attributes of a young adult. I had faced only adults who were sympathetic through the year.

My family nor I was prepared in any way for that day in court. We arrived at the courthouse and were escorted to a conference room. My grandmother was with us as well. At that point we were told that my parents would not be allowed in the courtroom with me. We were also told that we would be separated while I waited to testify. After some objection by my parents, the district attorney left and returned to say that while my parents would not be allowed in the courtroom—my grandmother could be present.

For the next period of time, which seemed forever, I sat on a hard bench in a tiny side room by myself. I had no idea where my parents were and could hear only muffled voices from inside the courtroom. Finally, a door opened, and I was asked into the courtroom. At that point, the judge asked if I knew what it meant to tell the truth, and explained that I would be put under oath. I raised my hand and felt grown up as I stepped into the chair. I had told myself repeatedly that it was important just to tell what had happened and not to let myself get too embarrassed. I was determined not to cry. There was no jury. Mr. McGlean had waived his right to a jury trial. The judge would make the decision.

The prosecuting attorney asked me to describe in detail what had happened. My shield of protection was to show no emotion. I finished my description, and the prosecuting attorney asked me no questions. The judge instructed me that I was to answer questions of the defense attorney with 'yes' or 'no'. I was not to elaborate. The defense attorney then asked me two questions:

Did Mr. McGlean hit you?
Answer: No

Did Mr. McGlean threaten to hit you?
Answer: No

The judge then excused me.

When I exited the courtroom, my parents were waiting for me. They looked surprised that I was already there. I no sooner sat down on the hard bench beside them when the bailiff exited the courtroom and announced that Mr. McGlean had been found 'not guilty as charged.'

All hell broke out. My father burst into the courtroom to try to reach the man who had caused so much injury. There was total chaos, and I disintegrated in a pool of tears. I heard the judge tell my father to calm down, or he would be held in contempt.

After several minutes the judge came and kneeled down next to me. I was sobbing. He said to me, "I want you to know that there was no question about whether you were telling the truth. But he didn't hit you. I can't find him guilty of assault."

Never mind that this man had taken me out on a dark road twenty miles from home. Where there was no chance that someone would hear me if I screamed. Where I heard my mother's voice telling me to stay calm so that he would not panic. Whether he had threatened me or hit me – I knew I was in danger, and there was only one way out. Never mind. No one asked me – neither the prosecutor nor the defense.

I listened intently as the judge talked with me. Then, he stood and started down the hall. As my family made an effort to calm me – I turned my head to watch the judge leave.   What I saw would be etched in my memory.   The judge was walking down the hall with his arm over Mr. McGlean's shoulder.   At thirteen, I understood that this was a sad example of justice and evil.

My parents were almost hysterical at that point as well.   The prosecutor wanted to talk with them.   My grandmother stepped up and said she was going to take me to a movie.   When we stepped outside, she said to me, "Susan, there is only one thing for you to know.   This man is sick.   No matter what happened today, it is important for you to know that what happened to you had nothing to do with love or the way a man will care for you one day.   Do not let this destroy you."   Those were wise words which I understood at one level but were not necessarily easy to live.

Later in the evening, my parents said that the explanation given to them was that there was no child molestation law in Florida.   That Mr. McGlean had gotten off on a technicality in the way the judge had interpreted the question of assault – based on whether Mr. McGlean had hit me. My father took it further.   He was convinced that the judge had been bought off.   It would eat at him for years.

There was now a new shame visited upon me.   Not only did I not understand why this man had molested me.   Now, I would take on the burden of a lost conviction.   When I burst out crying after the bailiff announced the verdict, my mother turned to me, one of the few times that she ever ridiculed me, and said, "Why didn't you do that in the courtroom?"   I thought I had been brave – the little warrior fighting for justice – that I had answered the questions as the judge told me.   Instead, it seemed as though I had let everyone down.   It would be years before events would allow me to sort out what had occurred and to realize fully that I was a child out on a dark road at the mercy of a sick person.   The Lord was with me that night. And I survived.

The assault against me was a classic case of a corrupt individual using his power and station in the evilest way possible. The journey to forgiveness would be a long hard road.

Our beloved Dr. Shepherd would see me in the next few weeks following that awful court decision and make a vow to me. "Susan," he said, "I promise you I will get a molestation law passed in this state. You did the right thing. And it will make it harder for this man to do this again. In any case, I will see to it that this doesn't happen to others."

Dr. Shepherd kept his word. He went to law school—became a judge—and eventually a state legislator. And he introduced and saw passed—one of the strongest child molestation laws in the country. Years later a colleague would describe to me that his daughter had been molested, and the perpetrator sent to jail for many years. This father and daughter had realized justice in the State of Florida. Later I would also have the opportunity to serve on a committee to provide a safe and friendly environment for children waiting to testify in court in Los Angeles. I considered it a gift that I had the opportunity to keep others from going through some of the fear and isolation I had felt so many years before.

I slowly began to experience that God's good does, in fact, come to all things. I cannot answer the question as to whether – at the times that we only feel agony – it is because we have blocked God's presence in our lives – or whether we are called upon to hang on the cross as our Lord. I can only witness that I felt God grieve with me, grant me grace, and reach down to provide direction. Eventually, I would resolve that I would not let the bad guys win by my turning away from the Lord, no matter the seeming injustice.

CHAPTER 8
Reconciliation

———◆———

"Be kind and compassionate to one another, forgiving
each other, just as in Christ God forgave you."

EPHESIANS 4:32

BETWEEN THE AGES OF FIFTEEN and thirty--life in many ways had almost
a fairy tale quality through many wonderful experiences.   I was a teenager attending a highly competitive high school and my natural zest for
life served me well. I won a national contest, married, had our beautiful
children, worked as a staffer in the US Congress and subsequently in the
White House, and was given opportunities to pursue many dreams and
passions.

However, in quiet moments of distress—that ugly question—had
I disappointed God—why had I been molested—had I done something
wrong—why did Mr. McGlean do what he had done—would surface in my
innermost thoughts. My self-doubts were never too far from the surface.

The day would come in my early thirties when my marriage was in
difficulty, and I would enter counseling. There was an array of issues.
However, several months into sessions the counselor would ask me a simple question. It would prove to be the doorway to many answers and

perhaps one of the most astounding conversations of my life. Proof, that in Christ, two people can find a path to forgiveness and reconciliation.

The question from the counselor was, "Why, at times, don't you feel that you deserve to be loved?" From somewhere, that I did not even know, that deep dark secret and dialog of self-shame emerged. I immediately answered, "Because of me my family lost everything." I was thirty-two at that point. I was molested at age twelve.

Over the next period of months, the counselor and I looked at the various aspects of what had occurred and how I had assimilated the events. We looked at the details from my point of view as a child—and now— years later as an adult.

The point of the discussions was to help me see, as an adult, that I had been under the control of an individual who separated me from my parents and then, at least outwardly, left me powerless. In fact, I had found power in my mother's voice in my head – and in the sense of danger, I felt before getting into Mr. McGlean's car. These answers were helpful to me but did not go far enough.

On my own, I decided to call the district attorney's office in Miami, to ask questions about what had taken place in my case. I reached a young assistant DA, who did not hesitate to be helpful.

I described to him the day that we had gone to trial. His reaction was – that even at that time – 1957 – that he could not imagine my separation from my parents at age thirteen.

My description of seeing the judge leave the court with his arm over the shoulder of the man who molested me was horrifying to him. I gave permission for him to unseal my files and he said that he would call me back. In a matter of days, he called back to tell me that he could not provide anything specific about my case – but that in fact – the judge in my case had been removed from the bench for taking bribes. There seemed little doubt that the outcome of my case had been predetermined. My father had said for years that he believed the judge had been paid off. It became apparent that his instincts had probably been correct.

At least the first part of the puzzle that continued in my head for so many years, namely, was my perception correct that the justice system failed me miserably, had been answered for me. I then asked whether it would be inappropriate for me to try to find Mr. McGlean and ask why he had done what he had done. The DA's response was surprising. It was that he encouraged people who had been victimized as children to confront the perpetrator as an adult for answers. He said that I should make it clear that I was not trying to do personal harm or to extort money. I was only looking for answers.

There is no doubt for me that the Lord's hand was once again upon me. I, at the time, lived in Washington, D. C. I called Miami information and did not find a listing for Mr. McGlean. After all, it was now twenty-two years later. My thought was that if he no longer was in Miami, that I was sure he was in the south. I thought that I remembered that he had owned a large sea freight business at one time. Out of 'the blue' I thought to call New Orleans information. And there was his name.

I dialed the number – a cheerful teenage voice answered the phone. She sounded as though she was about the age that I was when I was molested. I asked for Mr. McGlean. She responded, "Do you mean my father or my grandfather." I asked for her grandfather.

A few minutes later her father answered the phone. I identified myself by my maiden name and prefaced my questions by stating that I was not calling to cause problems but to seek answers. I asked Mr. McGlean's son whether he remembered that I had testified against his father.

At that moment the Lord was present with both of us. Without hesitation, Mr. McGlean's son stated that, of course, he remembered me. He went on to say that his father was dead. He asked what I wanted to have answered. I told him that I was hoping to put the years of self-doubt and questions to rest. That I was calling to ask his father why he had done what he did.

With that Mr. McGlean's son said to me:

"Susan, we all always loved you. My mother was heartsick. She cried for weeks and weeks. The answer to your question is that you were at the wrong place at the wrong time. Once I was an adult, I was able to stop my father. We moved from Miami because we were afraid someone would kill him. You were the only one who ever came forward in the courts, but we had to move to keep him from being killed. He bought his way out other times. We kept him under total lock and key during the last part of his life. He did this to others. There was nothing that you did to cause anything to happen."

What a liberating moment for my parents and me. My father no longer had to take on the guilt of failing to protect me. I no longer had to wonder about the whys. It truly was a liberating moment of grace.

My conversation ended with Mr. McGlean's son by both of us wishing each other well. We thanked God for bringing us together. I believe that that moment was as much a blessing for Mr. McGlean's son as it was for me. He had been granted the grace to make it right with me. He had the courage to stand up and take that opportunity.

I could, at that point, find reconciliation with myself, and with the Lord, for that time in my life. I would understand, as time went on, that this gift also gave me the responsibility to reach out, when possible, to help prevent situations for others or to seek assistance for others in that situation. I was able to turn from being a victim to being an advocate and a voice at times, for others who found no support from their families or found no means to stand up for themselves.

This son – who still showed compassion for his father – nonetheless did not defend his actions. I heard only relief in his voice as we ended our conversation. In the following days and weeks, I would feel the weight lifted from my shoulders.

I kept the light on an entire night in a bedroom without locks on the door. There was no guarding against the entry of Mr. McGlean — who despite the presence of his wife just steps away – came back that night for a second go round of tyranny over a twelve-year-old. His wife had baked an apple pie for my arrival. I will never know whether she was aware of what was taking place in the room steps away from where she supposedly was sleeping. Whatever the truth, I would ultimately know that it was up to me to forgive him for his actions; and to forgive either her ignorance or her silent complicity as well.

Naturally, I wonder who went before me – and even after me. There were whisperings of people in our old neighborhood who later would admit that they knew something was amiss. But no facts. Had I not been supported by everyone around me – from my father and mother to Dr. Shepard and the district attorney's office – I would not have found the courage to walk into a courtroom at age 13. It was through faith and my efforts to draw close to the Lord that I received the gift of reconciliation. And through the process, legislation was passed to bring accountability and justice for others.

I have not used this man's real name because of his son and his grandchildren. There is no purpose to be served by making his grandchildren, and possibly by now, great grandchildren bear the cross of his wrongs.

Between 1992, and 2010, there has been a 56% decline in physical abuse in the United States, thanks to the increasing spotlight on these crimes. However, a staggering 39 million adults in the United States today are estimated to have been molested or raped as children. Fewer than 20% of rapes are estimated to be reported each year. On average, 200,000 to 300,000 rapes are reported. The annual cost of rape is estimated at $127 billion. The real cost for victims and their families is far beyond that in emotional and life costs.

I give thanks for the grace bestowed upon me with the possibility of reconciliation. To forgive as I have been forgiven. I also give thanks that the Lord spoke to me before I got into that car—and that I would understand His guiding hand in the future.

CHAPTER 9

Between Nerd and Beauty Queen

———◆———

MOST OF US KNOW THE moments of struggle which have brought us to the feet of the Lord. But how many of us recognize the moments when God opens the way that creates a whole new direction for our lives? Isn't that what occurred with each of the Apostles? I have experienced several of those moments in my life. I, like most of us, at least initially, may have ignored, questioned, avoided or put off taking a step or action—which in hindsight was a huge blessing offered out of grace.

While this may seem like a silly first example—it influenced my life as much in a positive way—as being molested impacted my life in a negative way. In my sophomore year of high school—I followed a path which had not even remotely been on my radar.   A random homeroom announcement struck a chord. The principal announced that a new organization was starting at the school called Junior Achievement. The principal mentioned that it was a national organization which taught students about forming companies--with competitions and travel across the country to participate with other schools in a national convention. It provided opportunities for scholarships.

Junior Achievement was not known in my school. It was not popular. It simply wasn't in the regular education equation.

On the morning of that first announcement, I knew that I wanted to be one of those who went to a national JA convention. I allowed myself to be led down this path which was nerdy, in which none of my friends was participating and which I couldn't explain to anyone. Nor did I feel the need to justify my interest.

For three years, I participated in this organization that teaches teen-agers about the free enterprise system by forming small companies and selling products. It was an unduplicated opportunity, as major businesses sponsored Junior Achievement, with senior executives giving their time voluntarily every week to mentor teens through the school year. Each year of my participation resulted in life long relationships and tremendous opportunities.

From day one, I had enthusiasm for the sense of camaraderie with my team. We learned how businesses are formed and built a small company. Business leaders gave their time, to foster an appreciation and understanding of the basics of running a business; and globally – a better understanding of the free enterprise system.

That one moment in time – I can look back and know that the hand of the Lord touched me. It might seem silly to some. However, I am aware that there was an inner force which urged me on. The reality is that it changed my life. In August, 1962, I was named Miss Junior Achievement of the United States. Doors opened – mentors came forward – and I learned that following that still small voice would serve not only – as a shield of safety or as a door to personal success – but most importantly – for me to be used—in the future— as an instrument of the Lord.

During my year as Miss JA, I appeared as the 'real' Susan Ward on the TV game show "To Tell The Truth", often spoke at Rotary and Kiwanis Clubs, and hopefully, had a positive influence on other teenagers who might benefit from Junior Achievement. I would give back later by going back each year as a counselor at Indiana University, serving on local boards of JA, and overseeing efforts which were for the benefit of teenagers nationwide.

1964 Indiana University
Connecticut Governor
John Davis Lodge
President of Junior Achievement

1962- Indiana University
named Miss Junior Achievement
of the United States

I would also get a bird's eye view of larger events, when in 1962, Senate Candidate Ted Kennedy came to Miami, to make a statement on behalf of President Kennedy, on the Bay of Pigs.

Ted Kennedy was present, not as an individual, just 30 at the time, but as a young man representing the President of the United States. Events were leading to the Cuban missile crisis.

I was working for two weeks in the Junior Achievement press office at the event at which he was speaking. My role was to field phone calls for him for several hours while he was in Miami. A merry prospect for a senior in high school.

Miami, Fla. – Senate candidate Ted Kennedy

In the next couple of months, America would live through the tense days of the missile crisis, when planes were continuously overhead in Miami, as they moved out of range of a possible strafing attack from Cuba.

My family had visited Cuba, while Castro was still only a rebel. We had seen the barbed wire fences around homes and armed guards. My family, along with so many others, would soon be saddened to learn that Castro's liberation effort would degenerate into another form of fifty years of dictatorship for the Cuban people.

Close to twenty years after being named Miss JA of the US, I was serving as Special Assistant to the US Comptroller of the Currency in Washington, D.C. When President Reagan was elected, the newly named Secretary of the Treasury, Donald Regan, requested that I serve on the new Treasury transition team. He had been a national sponsor and Board member of Junior Achievement—and someone mentioned to him in passing—that I had been a member of JA, a counselor and a local Board member. All because on that one morning in high school, while joking with friends in homeroom, I felt I was being urged internally to follow up on a seemingly unimportant school announcement.

At seventeen, I cannot claim that I was acutely aware of the distinction between an internal drive combined with faith and being led or used by the Holy Spirit. I believe that is something that is revealed over time. When we take ourselves out of the way—with faith—we will have eyes to see and ears to hear. It is the willingness of spirit to be led by the Lord that allows the Holy Spirit to work through us. In mere self-absorption and inattention to our faith, we miss the messages and opportunities for grace which abound in our lives.

Mathew 6:24 "No one can serve two masters."

Through the years, I have referred to the action of God in my life as just that. Sometimes as the Lord in my life. Over time, I began to understand the doctrine of the Trinity—the Father, Son, and Holy Spirit—gaining a better understanding of the blessing of the indwelling Holy Spirit. In faith, we all may be blessed by being moved by the Holy Spirit and be blessed with gifts of the Spirit working through us.

At the age of twelve, I believe I was warned not to step into the car with a trusted individual who ultimately caused me great injury. At fifteen, I believe, in the midst of an ordinary day, I was moved by that still small voice, which led to many opportunities to accept God's gifts in my life—and to serve others. By whatever name, it is total faith in the saving grace of Jesus, and the willingness to hear and to act on the still small voice for good that opens the way to be led.

CHAPTER 10

Travel to Destiny or Unintended Consequences

———◆———

A FOUNDATION OF LOVING PARENTS and a strong conscience at an early age. The blessings and grace of faith at a young age. Learning to deal with pain well before my childhood was over. The opportunities that a good education affords. Seemingly all of the tools for basically good decision making.

The only thing lacking was a crystal ball.

There comes a point in almost everyone's life when one realizes that right decisions do not always turn out well. And that bad decisions do not always end badly. We can look at statistics, analyze, pray, and know that the odds are for us or against us in any given endeavor. And yet, the outcome may be different than expected. (Someone once defined a statistician to me as a person who looks at two pregnant women and two men standing on a corner, and describes them as four people fifty percent pregnant.)

At twenty-one, I served as Executive Secretary to the Director of Insurance at Trans World Airlines headquarters in New York. Late in the afternoon on November 20, 1967, word came that a TWA Convair had crashed on landing at Cincinnati Airport. By the time word came in, most of the staff had left for the day. Each of us remaining was given three names to telephone to notify next of kin that their family member was on board the crashed plane. Each of our calls was immediately followed by a call from an executive officer at TWA if we reached a relative. As the investigation and follow-through took place over the days following the crash, a profound sense of sadness fell over the entire staff at the headquarters. It seemed almost as though we all felt a sliver of responsibility. At all levels, whether by executives or by clerks, sorrow was felt for the loss of life that day. Unfortunately, I would again be tasked with breaking tragic and sad information to families.

At twenty-two, I married Bill Wagner. We were married for eleven years. It was during those years that our lives were impacted beyond what we could have imagined where our children were concerned. While we have been divorced for many years, we have never set aside the fact that we have been parents to two magnificent sons. I agreed to follow Bill to the ends of the earth when we were married. He had completed five years as an officer in the Marine Corps and was in law school. We met in Manhattan while campaigning on the Rockefeller Gubernatorial Campaign in New York. We were both idealistic, drawn to the national debate over the war in Viet Nam, and attracted to the Governor. I did not find out that Bill had applied and accepted a job at the State Department until we were well down the path in our relationship. However, reflecting the idealism of the 1960's, we were both ready to serve our country wherever we were sent.

At the time we were married, we moved to Washington, and I was offered a job as a research assistant for Congressman John Dellenback, a Republican from Oregon. I was twenty-two years old, and I was like a sponge soaking up information on the various issues facing the Congress and the country.

My role was to prepare position papers for the Congressman on legislation working its way through the Congress. I was fortunate that I was working for a man of integrity who instructed me to provide him with as complete a picture as possible of the influences on legislation, the facts related to proposed laws and the possible outcomes of the passage of laws. Before long I was promoted to Legislative Assistant and given individual case work.

It was a time in the country when bipartisanship was not a dirty word. The Congress was focused more on dealing with issues than with party politics. It would be naive to think that politics were set aside. Watergate was around the corner. However, the country was decidedly moderate rather than partisan. I loved my job.

On January 28, 1968, North Korea captured the USS Pueblo, killing young Duane Hodges, and holding the ship's crew captive. Duane Hodges was from Congressman Dellenback's district in Oregon. The Congressman immediately reached out to Duane's parents. Almost every day over the next 335 days of the crew's captivity, I made daily calls to the Defense Department, State Department and CIA to find out whether there were any significant events and the status of negotiations for the return of Duane's body. I would then give an update to the Congressman, and either he or I would call Duane's parents to provide them an update. He felt it was not possible to give too much attention to assisting them.

It was the first time in my young life that threats and events of the world were brought home to the core of my being. Each day I could feel the agony of Duane's parents, in knowing their son had died for his country, and that they were helpless to bring him home.

The Hodges' faith, patience and belief in the efforts of the US government served as a beacon to all of us. Their humility was at times overwhelming. At one point, I sat down on a bench on a sidewalk and sobbed over the senseless cruelty that was taking place. And while the politics, the posturing, and the negotiations swirled around them, each morning they thanked me for whatever little tidbit of information I might give them. Their son had his whole life ahead of him. He had planned to return to his family farm and the friends he had known all of his life. I never heard one word of complaint from the Hodges that their son had died in service to his country.

On April 4, 1968, the Reverend Dr. Martin Luther King was assassinated.

I was a bride of about four months and we were living on Capitol Hill. My new husband was away five days a week in a training program. We had rented a tiny apartment in a town house steps away from the Capitol and the Longworth House Office Building where I worked. I walked to work and many days came home for lunch. It was not unusual for us to go over to the office building to watch a nighttime hearing on an important piece of legislation. It was awe-inspiring to live a few steps away, as well, from the US Supreme Court Building and the Library of Congress. I felt a deep sense of pride in my country and appreciation for those who took service to the country, whether as a civilian or in the military, seriously.

The ugly vector of racism led to Dr. King's assassination. Capitol Hill was quickly turned into an armed camp as demonstrations and fires began to take hold in Washington. Tanks lined our street.

At that time, I had volunteered one night a week at the 'Receiving Home' in Washington. The name belied the fact that it was a maximum security juvenile detention institution. One side of the facility housed teenagers who were, generally, already hardened criminals at young ages. They were serious offenders waiting for trials.

The other side of the home was different. The other end housed a diverse group of children, under the age of ten, who had no real criminal history, who in all probability would not see the inside of a courtroom. Generally, at most, they were acting out because of their turbulent and uncontrollable circumstances.

I volunteered to do an arts and crafts program with the children. The Director of the Receiving Home had explained to me that by and large, the children were picked up off the street, sometimes fairly neglected, and brought to the Receiving Home so that they would have a short period of warm meals and a safe bed in which to sleep. The Director was committed to making the effort to mentor those children, giving them a safe place and hopefully finding nurturing circumstances or support. He had been clear with me that it was important, that if I started the program, that I remain committed to my one night a week so that the kids could count on me. They generally had few people in their lives on whom they could count. I found them lively, enthusiastic about the arts program and responsive to my efforts.

The Receiving Home was located in the heart of northeast Washington—in the heart of demonstrations and fires in response to Dr. King's death. There was brief concern about my going into that part of Washington, on the night after the African American leader's death.

The whole African American community was harmed in that one act. Whether we knew it or not, so too was the rest of America. I found myself asking myself how I could let down this one small group who might have benefited, however remotely, from the leadership shown by Dr. King. I decided to go ahead.

The night seemed little different when I first arrived. However, it soon became apparent that the children knew and understood what had happened the night before. As I searched for how I might best give comfort to these youngsters, one of the boys, no more than eight years old, stepped up to me and took my hand. His words, "It's all right Miss Susan. We know you are not like them. You're not like the ones who hate us." All I could do was give him a hug and say to him that I hoped he would never meet anyone who hated him. I went on to express that it was terrible that Dr. King had been killed. I would think of the fact, through many years, that this beautiful small child—on a night when he might have learned about hatred—sought to give comfort to me. However insignificant in the total scheme of things, I was thankful that I had not let this small group down that night.

In August 1968, I took a one week leave from my job as legislative assistant to Congressman Dellenback, to attend the Republican Convention, working on behalf of then Governor Nelson Rockefeller, for president. In the aftermath of the nomination of Richard Nixon, to be the Republican candidate for President, I was present, as a behind the scenes effort was mounted, for a floor fight at the convention.

An effort was underway to nominate Nelson Rockefeller, as Vice President, rather than Spiro Agnew. My role was to call Republican Senators and Representatives to organize an effort led by Senator Charles Goodell. For several hours it appeared that the course of history might be altered. And I witnessed a group of men who were ready to put their entire careers on the line to do what they felt was right for the country. The effort was quashed by the Governor himself, as he felt strongly that it was the prerogative of Richard Nixon to make his choice for Vice President. They treated the matter with dignity and respected Governor Rockefeller's decision.

Governor Nelson Rockefeller 1968

Shakespeare's "to thine own self be true" has come to have many different meanings for people. For me, it is to make the decisions that match my faith, values, beliefs, and goals. And thereby, to take responsibility, hopefully with a humble heart, for my failures as well as my successes.

I have, at times had an overblown sense of empowerment. Some might call it youth. Overall, I give thanks for the strength and optimism which seemed to be an inherent part of my being. It has served as a catalyst for me to step out of the ordinary at times, matched my inborn sense of adventure, and helped me avoid the horrendous pitfall of blaming God for my mistakes. I give thanks that I do not have to try to crawl out of a hole of derision, shame, self-loathing, and blame. There is only one reason that I can do this. Through faith in the Lord.

In the two years before we left for Africa, I encountered three different situations where lives were lost as the result of tragedies. Many families experienced the tragedy, the pain, the courage, the depth of faith and reality of God's love and good that came to each of the situations. Passengers boarded a plane, a flight that ended tragically; a young man volunteered to serve his country and gave his all; and an American leader presented the world with his vision and dreams that would live on past his tragic death. In a fourth instance, a group of men had to make a decision about whether to try to change the course of history. The reality is that none of us ever knows whether we are on a journey to destiny or unintended consequences. Only in faith, however, can we always know that we are in God's hands.

Until April 2000, after Christian died, I told people that I would not trade the experience of serving in Africa, despite many challenges at times. The day came when it became apparent that a great deal had been at stake. For years, having only begun to understand the implications of our decisions, I sometimes referred to our years in Africa, as our too young and too dumb to know better years.   However, they were also the years when we were blessed with our children, when there was deepening of faith, where we felt our service to our country had a meaningful impact, and where we viewed and learned about the world beyond the confines of family, community, and country.

CHAPTER 11

Challenges and Blessings

———◆———

"Every good and perfect gift is from above.."

JAMES 1:17

WE WERE AMONG THE FIRST families assigned to the Congo, after what was known as the Stanleyville massacre of 1964. Before the successful takeover of the army by President Joseph Mobutu, members of the US Consulate had died, along with many others, in a rebel attack in Stanleyville. The country had been in disarray for some years after that. For several years, American families were not assigned to the embassy, which was located approximately fifteen hundred miles away from Stanleyville, in Kinshasa, the capitol of the Congo. But it was a difficult post for a foreign service officer to weather without a family.

As the country stabilized, it was important for the Embassy to be fully staffed. The State Department went a long way to ensure that those assigned to the area were able to acclimate to embassy living and the foreign culture. We attended the Foreign Service Institute, took French on a concentrated basis and prepared ourselves for our assignment. The Embassy was one of the larger ones in West Africa, at that time, and there was a decent US military presence. It would turn out that there was also a compatible American and diplomatic community. As was true for our counterparts in the States, who were in their twenties and thirties, our free time was spent enjoying swimming, tennis, volleyball, occasional visits to local clubs, and occasional trips to the interior of the Congo or other nearby countries. There was lots of camaraderie and spirit within the embassy.

I accepted the challenges of living in the Congo with relative ease. There were daily influences and events — which were outside the norm of our culture but with vigilance they were manageable. At times I thought of myself almost as the equivalent of a pioneer woman, facing the challenges of snakes, malaria, and potential rebel activity. I was dedicated to our well-being and participation in all aspects of the culture and country. We made friends quickly with our Congolese neighbors and prided ourselves as caring Americans. We remained in the Congo for three and a half years. We felt it was a successful tour.

In the second year of our tour, we made the decision that it would be safe for me to become pregnant. I didn't become pregnant as quickly as I had hoped—and soon prayed that we would not have difficulty becoming parents. Our prayers were answered. And, no, I do not think that babies come just from prayers. Darling Will and Christian were born over the next two years in the formerly Belgian clinic in Kinshasa, managed by nuns.

I had easy pregnancies and by all standards, uncomplicated deliveries. I was given the choice, in my seventh month of pregnancy, each time, to evacuate to the American military base in Frankfurt, Germany, or to return to the States for three months to have my babies. Although the clinic was basic, and there would be no anesthesia during their births except in the case of extreme emergency, I was convinced that the doctors were dedicated and that I would be safe. We were thrilled to become parents, and I did not want to be separated during critical moments of our marriage. I chose to remain in Kinshasa, for both of their births.

I focused on eating in a healthy manner. I exercised regularly. I ordered multiple books on pregnancy and childbirth. For two months we practiced the Lamaze method on our own. I took advantage of the 100 degree plus temperatures in the afternoons to rest, and ultimately, to spend hours reading the Bible. Doing so just evolved. Initially, I wanted to look up a reference I had seen in a book. It went on to become the first time that I read the Bible from start to finish. The liturgy in the Episcopal Church includes a yearly calendar of the Bible, used in services and from which sermons are based. I had read individual chapters from time to time. But I had never sat, read, and prayed through the entire Bible. I would describe the process as one of quietness and comfort rather than one in which I felt profound new insights. It was not a mission of searching but rather one of just being.

Gloriously, our first son, Will, was born on November 6, 1970. He was a happy, healthy baby. We were joyful and thankful for his arrival. Each day was an incredible new adventure with him. He brought endless smiles to our faces.

There were no diaper services, throw away diapers, or even a reliable source of milk supply. We washed diapers in an old fashioned ringer washer, hung them to dry indoors and ironed them so there would be no exposure to parasitic white worms found in the trees outside. Even the larvae could be blown about and would infest the skin on contact. I had made the decision to nurse before ever becoming pregnant. I had a back-up supply of Carnation's evaporated milk in case there was a problem but there was not. All went as hoped.

We were so pleased with parenthood and the experience of childbirth in the small clinic in Kinshasa that we decided not to resume birth control after Will was born. Nursing proved to be a natural form of birth control, and we decided to let nature take her course. I nursed Will for nine months, adding food at different stages in his development. Eleven months later I became pregnant with Christian.

I had little morning sickness with Will. In my second pregnancy, I had even less. I felt great from the beginning. However, I developed uneasiness. I did not know why. It is a question which will never be answered but has returned to my thoughts many many times throughout the years. Will, was a happy bouncing boy who was all about exploring the world, laughing, and bringing joy to our lives. In our eyes he was perfect. There did not appear to be any reason for concern.

In about the third month of pregnancy with Christian, I began to have thoughts of whether we would be so blessed to have another healthy baby. There was no basis for my concern. I kept reminding myself that things had gone well with Will's birth. However, the feeling grew. I wound up writing a letter to my sister asking her whether she had had feelings of concern during her pregnancy with her second son. She answered that at times with both of her babies she had had moments of concern. She reassured me that it was normal to have various thoughts during pregnancy. As long as I was healthy and there were no signs of difficulty that she would consider those ideas mainly a part of changing hormones.

During the nine months, however, two events were different than with Will. First, during the entire time we were in the Congo, we had had to take chloroquine to prevent malaria. We had begun taking it weeks before our departure to the Congo, continued it through my pregnancy with Will, through vacations out of the country. We were cautioned that we should continue it for an extended period beyond our final departure from the Congo. Malaria remains in the system for several months and is not suppressed if chloroquine is discontinued too soon. Will had been put on small doses from the beginning as well. He showed no side effects from taking it.

In the early 1970's, in the Congo, there was no television and no internet. Thus I was not bombarded with dire warnings about the effects of chloroquine during pregnancy. However, I became concerned about whether my uneasiness could be because of taking the malaria prophylaxis. Since I was not spending time outdoors in areas where I was subject to a lot of mosquito bites—and did not have any mosquito bites — I made the decision to reduce the recommended dosage. Within weeks, during approximately my fifth month of pregnancy, I contracted malaria. Now, it was necessary to take large doses of chloroquine. I prayed that this would not cause me to go into labor or affect my dear baby. It did not. Fortunately, the symptoms dissipated within about ten days.

Then a threatening event occurred in my seventh month. I had eaten some imported crabmeat at an embassy party and felt fine. I had never had any reaction to eating crab. I did, however, have a deadly allergy to aspirin which developed when I was a teenager. I was warned that I should avoid it at all costs.

Suddenly, shortly after attending the embassy party, I developed massive hives and began to have breathing issues. We called the embassy doctor, and he immediately came to our home. He immediately administered cortisone but dared not give adrenaline given to me during previous allergic episodes. A question arose as to whether I might have been given aspirin without my knowledge. There simply was no way to know whether it was a sudden allergic reaction to the crab or whether, somehow, I had gotten a dose of aspirin. Now, my worst fears were realized—as the doctor warned that the next few hours would be crucial—and that there was a possibility that I might go into labor.

I did not go into labor and over the next few days the swelling of my eyes, face and hands receded. One of my former husband's colleagues came to the house right after I broke out in the hives and almost fainted when he saw me. It was not a pretty sight.

Sweet Christian Read Wagner was born after a short labor, on August 30, 1972. He was as beautiful as Will, and a wonderfully happy, healthy and joyful baby. We could not have been more blessed.

Despite occasional reports of unrest, we were comfortable in the Congo. We appreciated local customs, related well to both the African and European communities and felt a sense of service to our country. We, therefore, felt prepared to take a post for another two years in West Africa. We were well briefed when we were next assigned to Guinea, that it was considered one of the most difficult hardship posts in the foreign service. However, after three and a half years in the Congo, we felt we were well prepared for whatever lay ahead.

Up to this point it would seem that I had made acceptable decisions. At twenty-seven, I had held responsible jobs typically filled by individuals beyond my age. I had married a person who was well respected. I had served my country both in Washington and abroad. And I had two beautiful sons. Life in the foreign service allowed me to be a stay at home mom and to love the moments that I spent with my kids. I loved nurturing them, playing with them, and using my creativity to provide an enjoyable environment for them. It would seem that I had made good life choices.

As we made the joint decision to accept the next post in Conakry, Guinea, we were well aware that the circumstances were considered challenging. In the Congo, President Mobutu had realized sustained power in part due to the backing of the American government and was decidedly pro-American. We were also present under the umbrella of the Geneva Conventions and diplomatic passports. While Americans had lost their lives in the Stanleyville massacre, and there were certain inherent dangers in the Congo, the general environment was friendly.

We entered the foreign service, first, with the assurance that our US leaders would always stand behind us. Second, that as a family we would not be sent into circumstances with unmanageable danger. And third, that in the case of immediate danger, that no cost or effort would be spared to retrieve us.

In going to Guinea, we knew that we were going into a different environment than the Congo. We were only ten or so Americans among hundreds of Russians, Chinese and Eastern bloc diplomats. The first president of Guinea, President Ahmed Sekou Torre had renounced the French, and all remnants of Guinea as a former French colony, as well as all American influence. He embraced a Marxist philosophy, and it was a Muslim country with many different tribal forces. He ruled with an iron hand, from 1958 until his death in 1984, and used all of the military and propaganda tactics for which the Russians were known during the cold war. Guinea was also the home to PLO trainees. And Guinea was one of the few places in the world where there were no US Marines in the embassy to provide any protection whatsoever.

Unlike the Congo, however, where Americans had lost their lives, there had never been any loss or injury to Americans serving in Guinea. While our lives might be less comfortable than desired, we were at ease answering the challenge to once again serve our country.

Will was twenty-six months old, and Christian was five months old when we boarded the plane to Guinea. Neither of them, of course, had a say so about our plans.

CHAPTER 12
Isolation

———————◆———————

BEFORE TRANSFERRING FROM THE CONGO to Guinea, we were given a three-month break back in the United States. It was both a vacation and time to adequately prepare ourselves for our new post. We planned carefully for Will and Chris, trying to anticipate as many of our requirements as possible for the next two years.

In the Congo, there was a central street market for fresh vegetables, two grocery stores with a good supply of canned goods and home supplies, and we had a once a week delivery by US military, if we chose to order food from neighboring South Africa. Apartheid was not yet over, and we chose not to support the repressive South African regime economically. We were able to buy what we needed off of the local economy in Kinshasa, and limited our orders from South Africa to emergency supplies in only a few circumstances. There also was a small American military PX available to embassy personnel. We could get some of our good ole American favorites like peanut butter, macaroni and cheese, and occasionally M&Ms. Just enough so that we didn't feel as though we had left all of our comforts of home.

While there were only a few stores for clothes, which were expensive, we had the military APO for small packages and mail delivery once a week. We kept ourselves well stocked in sportswear mainly out of the

Sears catalog and ordered a little more elegant attire from American based boutiques which would ship. It was also fun to purchase local African prints from which we made or had made simple blouses or dresses.

Our preparations for Guinea were far different. We knew that there were no locally operated stores in Conakry or the rest of the country. The general Guinean population ate mainly manioc, a variation of the yucca plant, indigenously grown fruit and fish that they caught themselves. It was against Guinean law for us to purchase anything from Guineans. We were never offered food, artifacts or any other products. We could buy limited amounts of gasoline with coupons from the embassy. There was not a single restaurant. There was theoretically one small diplomatic store operated by the Yugoslav embassy which mainly had empty shelves. Occasionally one could find a can of beans or some other delicacy for the equivalent of five or ten dollars. I once paid six dollars for one fresh onion. It was not necessary for me to carry money with me for two years because there was nothing to purchase.

Before leaving for Guinea, we ordered eight months of dry and canned food and supplies to be delivered from Amsterdam by ship to the port. We were given an allowance for a one time purchase of household goods at a military PX in Washington, for clothes, toys, etc. to be shipped from the States. Included in that shipment was a swing set for the kids. We also ordered the equivalent of a cow—of frozen meat to be shipped from a New York meat house to Guinea, which would arrive a couple of months after we arrived. We would be able to replenish our meat supply approximately every six months.

Fresh vegetables and eggs were flown into Guinea by commercial flight once a month, from Belgium They were expensive shipments. Locally, there were no fresh vegetable markets whatsoever or other means of obtaining food or any other supplies.

After a few months, I planted a small garden with tomatoes, lettuce and green beans with seeds I had brought from the states. The garden later was eaten in one afternoon by happy local goats who made their way through our gates.

All embassy personnel had rooms set aside in their homes to store their supplies. There were window air conditioners to keep the rooms chilled, and each family had two freezers to store the meat and other frozen items shipped from the States. There were noisy generators in the carport in case the electricity went off for extended days.

Whenever a shipment arrived from Europe or the States, it felt like Christmas. It was fun to open the cartons first without the inventory because invariably there were items that we did not remember ordering and they were delights to discover.

Just before our departure for Guinea, our family reported for our State Department physicals in Washington. It turned out that the doctor performing our physicals had served briefly in Guinea. Although there were only ten families in the embassy, we had a full-time physician as there was no other medical care available. It was a frustrating gig for the doctor. With only ten families in the entire embassy, there were not enough patients to occupy medical personnel even close to full time, and the Guinean government would not allow US doctors to treat anyone outside of the embassy. Occasionally someone from another embassy would fall ill, and they would sneak into the embassy to be treated by our doctor. For someone who had taken the Hippocratic oath, it was deeply disturbing to have to stand by and watch the local population die from basic diseases. President Sekou Torre's iron hand would not allow assistance from a US doctor.

The doctor doing our pre-departure physicals in Washington was delighted to have the opportunity to talk about Guinea, and our preparations for this new assignment. He had done a tour in the small capital two years before. The four of us were all in good health, so there were no obstacles to our departure. As we left his office, the doctor was shaking his head and laughing. "Just remember," he said. "No matter how terrible people tell you it is going to be, and how much they say how difficult it will be, remember one thing—it will be worse." I laughed cheerfully at his joke.

The ride from the airport in Conakry, to our new home was different than I had expected. I had been in numerous West African countries during our three and a half years in the Congo, and all of them had sections of their capital cities that were predominately African, with a westernized influence. As we drove from the airport, we saw virtually all huts. There were a few old and rusted trucks and cars. And there were groups of people with what looked like half starving cows and goats. Most of the houses were dilapidated. I noticed immediately that people along the way kept their eyes down. We were warned that we would see what appeared to be young boys with rifles who were charged with keeping order and checking strangers' identifications. We were in an embassy car with a Guinean driver, and at least initially, we were waved through the checkpoints. I remember thinking to myself that I wondered what it would be like to live in the midst of the huts and goats and chickens. And at that moment we turned into the long driveway of our new home. We were going to be living in the midst of the huts, and goats and chickens. I was all right with that.

We were told that we would be living in the house formerly occupied by American peace corps volunteers before they had been pulled out of the country for safety reasons. We also knew that the house was on the ocean and that it would have basic furnishings. It would have space for the swing set, and it was enclosed on the street side by a wall and a large gate. What we did not know was that after the peace corps volunteers had left, Guinean military had occupied the house for a period. So while it was spacious, we soon found that the kitchen had been completely removed, there were no security bars on the windows, and the yard was covered in thrown away bottles and scraps.

In Guinea, as in the Congo, all of our water had to be boiled and filtered. For the first several weeks we had only a hotplate on which to boil water or to cook meals. I was given repeated assurances by the embassy admin officer that our kitchen appliances would be replaced and that we were a high priority to receive security bars for our windows. We inherited an excellent cook from a family departing Guinea. We had a small army, including two housemen to clean and do laundry, a gardener, and a night watchman. Our cook would arrive late morning to prepare lunch and to bake bread. He would leave for a few hours after lunch and return late afternoon to make dinner. This life would seem quite glamorous except that each day had challenges that would require all of the resources available to keep our household functioning.

Once again we had a wringer washing machine and had to dry clothes indoors to prevent infestation by parasites. We were now living almost directly on the equator where temperatures were typically over 110 degrees. There was a seven-month monsoon season, so preventing mold was a round-the-clock endeavor. The utility infrastructure was nearly destroyed when the French had departed Guinea, so at the first sign of rain and an inevitable lightning strike, the electricity would cut off for hours. It was virtually a daily endeavor to move food around to be sure that perishable food in the refrigerator was not destroyed. While we had a generator, it was ancient and difficult to start. For daily outages, it was pretty much useless. In the hot temperatures, we'd often sit in the plastic kiddy pool we had brought, to keep both the kids and ourselves cool.

The positive side of the assignment was that I had plenty of time to spend with Will and Christian. For the first several months, when they were napping I worked in the yard with the gardener to remove debris left by the former military occupants. I had brought all kinds of arts and crafts materials, books, blocks and toys with us, so there was plenty to entertain them and for them to entertain themselves.

All of the above, however, was atmospheric. The reality of the vast difference in serving in an anti-American repressive country would soon begin to dawn on us. As in the Congo, there was no television, but there was radio. We soon discovered that each day there were constant warnings to the Guinean population about potential attacks from unknown invaders, followed by diatribes about the dangers of capitalism and American imperialists. There were repeated rallies calling for the death of Americans. We learned quickly not to listen to these rallies. We told ourselves that it was all propaganda with no teeth.

As in the Congo, most of our entertainment came in the form of luncheons and dinner parties at fellow Americans' homes and with a few other western diplomats. However, unlike the Congo, there was no external form of entertainment, except for an occasional gathering for a picnic and games with embassy personnel. In the Congo, we had many African friends both from the Congo and from other African embassies. The Guinean government did not allow large groups to congregate, and we were not authorized to have any contact with Guinean citizens. Guineans are gentle kind people, and it was sad to be in a country where someone might be arrested for having a conversation with us. Soon we also realized that for Guineans, the threat of disappearance for virtually any perceived infringement was real. We began to understand that when we heard the rumble of trucks during the night, it was likely that someone had disappeared. By the end of Sekou Torre's twenty-five years of rule, in 1984, thousands had disappeared, and thousands were incarcerated in concentration-like camps.

We had been warned that the government engaged in various types of harassment of American embassy personnel and their families. The harassment was against Geneva Conventions, but the attitude within the embassy was that there was a low level of actual danger. More or less regularly we would get word that our weekly mail delivery from the States was delayed as it was confiscated while being unloaded at the airport. As mail was our only means of contact with the outside world, we looked forward to our weekly deliveries with great anticipation. Within the first months of our arrival, the first seeds of isolation began to be effective.

We were forewarned that it was likely that our homes were bugged. We were careful about our conversations—occasionally saying things that were silly just for effect. Any meaningful conversation took place outside. Our phones were tapped as well, and on one occasion I received a call from the person listening to our calls, to tell me the destination of a friend when I told someone on the phone that I couldn't remember where the person had gone. We were extraordinarily careful not to have any conversations with any of our housemen that could in any way be misinterpreted. Despite that, we would later find out that our cook, a gentle man who in no way was political, was killed for his association with us.

There was only one main road to the Embassy from our homes. Four or five of us lived on one side of Conakry, and the others on the opposite side of what was known as the corniche. Dinner parties were early in the evening as there was a curfew that was strictly enforced. As the time drew close to curfew, we were likely to be stopped by teenagers with Russian provided rifles checking our identification. Often they would come to my side of the car with a gun pointed at me while my former husband handed over the required identification. My biggest fear was that the car would backfire or that someone would do something that would cause one of the boys to panic.

Within a few months of our arrival, I began to have extreme stomach pains and difficulty eating. It was couple of months before it was determined that I had contracted a parasite, by which time I was down to around 100 pounds.

I had to fight to get security bars on our windows—which happened only after we were awakened to the sound of breaking glass and burglars. The burglars had not only been in our bedroom. Their exit was through our boys' room.

There were almost semi-weekly events. A tank of propane exploded as I entered the kitchen, burning my face and my eyelashes and eyebrows. I was thrown across the room when I turned on the water in the kitchen with an apparently rat-chewed open electric wire in the wall, touching the pipe. I watched our food shipment disappear into the hands of Guineans, when the truck driving from the port to our home went off the road.

We heard a lot about the iron hand with which the Russian ambassador ruled the Russian embassy, but had not understood the implications. Americans were off limits to Russian personnel. It had not been unusual in the Congo, for members of the American and Russian Embassies to socialize. I was horrified to find that a simple act of hospitality on my part resulted in the wife of a Russian diplomat being confined to the Russian embassy for months. I had gotten into a conversation with her on the beach behind our house, and it never occurred to me that I would be putting her at risk by inviting her to bring her children to play with mine for a few minutes. Unfortunately, while she was in our home, a courier from an eastern bloc embassy came to the house to deliver an official document. He returned to his office and called the Russian Embassy to report her presence in our home. There was nothing funny about the anti-American sentiment, so foreign to anything in my previous experiences, traveling and living overseas.

There were now extended periods when there were only a couple of American wives left in the embassy. The Ambassador's wife spent many months in the States, and generally, one or two families were away. One spouse had decided that she would return to the States permanently. I was asked to teach kinder garden for a semester at the international school. It was a welcome distraction from the daily challenges of the environment. In a climate of increasing isolation, it gave me the opportunity to have contact with a handful of mothers from other embassies. I could take both Will and Christian with me to the small school. Again, because of the circumstances, supplies were limited and called for a certain amount of creativity to to provide the basic learning required in the curriculum. I enjoyed the contact with the dozen or so children, the principal, who taught the small grade school, and the other mothers.

Guinea is a Muslim country with several indigenous tribal religions. About 85% of the country is Muslim. About 5% of the country is Christian. Beginning in the late 1960's it was illegal to proselytize in any fashion. In 1971, the Guinean Roman Catholic Archbishop was sentenced to life in prison, having been accused of plotting against the State.

When we arrived in 1974, there was one American missionary couple in the country. They conducted a small Sunday service, and embassy personnel were asked to stay away from the service lest we put them in danger. In the interior of the country, there was also a French nun who had been in the country for forty-seven years. When she left to return to France, after forty-seven years of service, no Guineans were allowed to go to the airport to see her off.

The American missionary couple lived down the beach from us and over the two years that we were in Guinea, we quietly got to know them. They would come down the beach in the dark to spend a few minutes with fellow Americans. Eventually, I would use the diplomatic pouch to smuggle one Bible at a time to them. That afforded a risk to them and us. It came about through a quiet suggestion, and we never discussed the ramifications or possible consequences. When I received a Bible, I would take a walk down the beach during the day and barely nod at them. We would meet briefly later in the evening just long enough for me to hand the book to them. I never had any discussion with anyone in the embassy about it. And fortunately, no Bible arrived when our mail was confiscated.

As time passed, there were fewer and fewer excursions from home without the boys' father. I would make trips only to the Embassy and back on the one main road on which we were allowed to travel. Besides being burglarized, there were repeated episodes that demonstrated that no matter how closely we followed prescribed Guinean rules that we could not provide guaranteed safety for ourselves and our children.

On one occasion, as I returned from the Embassy, the main road was cut off. We had been warned that if we wandered off main roads, we could end up in military camps and that we could be shot on sight. On this day, there was no choice. The road was blocked, and there was no place to turn around. All I could do was to make a turn before I reached the soldiers ahead with rifles pointed at anyone who approached them.

Will and Christian were in the car with me. Will was sitting in the back seat, and Christian was sitting in his car seat. I turned onto a dirt road, with no idea of where it would lead. I hoped, that since it was the only place to turn before the road was blocked, that the soldiers had chosen that spot because they knew the road would go through. That was not exactly the case. Mine was the only car on the road, and I quickly realized that I was riding into the center of a military camp.

I made the decision that it would be best to keep going rather than stopping. The men appeared as surprised to see me as I was to be there and no one made an effort to stop me. I told Will to stand up and to start waving at the soldiers. I hoped that in seeing that there were children in the car that they would realize that I intended no threat. I kept my eyes straight ahead so that I would not make eye contact. Eventually, the dirt road did lead back to the main road where I could quickly return to home.

The need to stay off the road, most unfortunately, was re-enforced on a day when Will was riding with his father from the embassy to home. Just before reaching an overpass, with Will in the front seat, a Guinean man was publicly hung from the bridge. As Bill realized in horror what they were seeing, there was nothing he could do before Will got a glimpse. Today, at age 45, Will says that he does still remember the sight.

As our harassment continued, we became aware of the fate of many Guineans, dying of basic diseases, malnutrition, or incarceration by the government. According to UN statistics, the average life expectancy for Guineans, at that time, was thirty-five years. Meditation and writing became my solace. My centeredness came through sitting quietly in meditation and prayer, sometimes for as much as two hours at a time, by the ocean. While initially, it was an exercise to cope with isolation, the process became an ever-deepening spiritual process.

Unlike the Congo, where we had had close friends, and generally a positive atmosphere, Guinea was about mutual support among the few of us for surviving. We had to think of the possible significance of our actions and to be prepared for the unexpected from many different directions. Trying circumstances turned into opportunities for laughter as well. It was not unusual for us to appear at each other's door in robes with towels and soap in hand, having stepped into our showers, and soaped our hair, only to have our water turned off. We knew if the water was turned off on our side of the corniche, we could go to a fellow American's home on the other side to finish our shower.

As in the US Embassy in Benghazi, we had an iron vault at the embassy for potential refuge and short wave radios at home for emergency communications with each other. As absurd as it seems, we had a rowboat at the house with instructions that if I was given a particular code by shortwave radio, that I was to put my infant son and toddler son into the rowboat, and begin rowing in the Atlantic Ocean, towards Sierra Leon. Seriously.

My willingness to be in Guinea began to change with an off-hand remark by my then husband. He commented to me one day that in a case of emergency or catastrophe, his first obligation would be to the embassy and the Ambassador. In other words, I might be on my own, should an emergency occur. At the time, I understood his dedication. However, I began to think about life, almost solely in terms of the safety of our children. I would realize that most Americans have no idea of the level of dedication of embassy personnel overseas. There was little understanding of the real circumstances for Americans serving in difficult locations.

CHAPTER 13

Helpless in the Circumstance

———◆———

"Surrender your heart to God, turn to him in prayer."

JOB 11:13-15

DURING OUR YEARS IN THE Congo, we had been well inoculated against all types of diseases, and we were rarely around anyone with any infection. My stint with malaria was preventable and I, fortunately, recovered quickly from the effects. I had no further bouts with hives and both Will, and Christian were healthy.

Guinea proved to be a different animal. Despite boiling and filtering the water carefully, I contracted a temporarily debilitating parasite. And subsequently a virtually chronic ear infection. It eventually would have to be removed surgically, and at one point, I was flown to Germany for tests to determine whether I might have a brain tumor. I did not. However, I lost much of the hearing in my right ear for several years. The medical prognostication was that as long as I remained in Guinea, with its seven-month monsoon season, high humidity, and hot temperatures, I would continue to have to deal with ear infections.

Soon there would be a new threat. Rabies was rampant in Guinea. There were enormous palm rats and wild monkeys in the area, so we were always vigilant if we were outside. Several members of embassies had contracted rabies and died over a several year period, so we took the threat seriously. I was held at bay, in the car, one afternoon, as a wild monkey sat on the windshield of my car entertaining himself. It did not show signs of illness, but I was not taking any chances.

At the Yugoslav operated store that I visited on occasion, there was a domesticated baby chimpanzee. He loved to be held and would come to people as they stepped out of their cars — asking to be picked up. He loved to be bounced like a baby, and it was fun to hold him. One afternoon I had Will with me when I stepped out of the car. I was carrying him on my hip when the chimpanzee walked up. I called him by name and had no concern. He looked as though he was reaching for me to pick him up as well. However, as I leaned down he proceeded to sink his teeth into Will's leg and bite down as hard as he could.

His owners quickly grabbed him, and we headed straight to the embassy doctor, Cory Snow. It was a painful bite. There was little the doctor could do to stop the pain at that moment. And there was a greater threat. Was the little chimpanzee sick or simply jealous? Because rabies was so rampant there was no time to wait for him to be quarantined to make a determination. Our doctor explained that the shots do not prevent rabies. Rather the inoculations contain an inactivated rabies virus which then causes the body to initiate its defenses. If the virus reaches the brain before the system has developed its immunity, rabies will develop. He felt it was fortunate that the bite was on Will's leg with a longer development time for infection.

Will would have to have a series of eight shots. Typically, in an adult, they would be given in the stomach. That is so that there is no subcutaneous scar tissue from a lifetime of shots in the hip. Cory felt that in Will's case, he did not need to put them in his stomach. But they would have to go in different locations in his hips, buttocks, and legs. They would be painful. Cory did not want Will to associate going to the embassy with the pain, so he suggested that he bring the shots each day to the house.

Bill would hold Will in his arms as Cory gave the shot so that he would not have to be lying down.

The shots were as bad as we thought they would be. Each time Will was given a shot, it was so painful that it would take Will's breath away. He would start to cry, and no sound would come out at first. All we could do was hold him and comfort him until the pain subsided. Each time a large welt would develop—a sign that the vaccine was working.

The incubation period for rabies can be from one week to three months. It would be weeks before Cory felt it reasonable to assure us that there was no chance that Will was in danger. The chimpanzee was shipped off and as far as we ever knew—never developed rabies. Once he was gone, we were not able to obtain any reports on him.

I, of course, was angry with myself that I had not thought about the potential danger for Will. I love animals and delighted that the chimpanzee liked for me to pick him up. There was another family in the embassy who had a baby chimpanzee and there had never been any problem when we were at their home. That was little consolation. I had to get it through my head that any unusual situation had the potential for causing difficulty. That's just the way it was.

We had always known that if there was any unusual illness that we would have to be evacuated. Cory had a supply of antibiotics, means of setting broken bones, and could perform minor surgeries. There was a very competent Scottish nurse, the wife of an independent construction contractor, who assisted Cory in giving shots and tracking required vaccines for embassy personnel. In a case of extreme emergency, however, it would be necessary for the embassy to gain clearance for an American military plane to land to enable an evacuation.

One evening Christian began to run a low temperature. He was a bit cranky and did not have much of an appetite. He woke up several times during the night, and I rocked him until morning.

The next morning, we were off to the embassy to see Cory. Other than a red throat he did not see much that was unusual, and we returned home with instructions to give him baby aspirin if he ran a temperature. Through the day Christian worsened. By the end of the afternoon, he was running a temperature of 101 and crying almost continually. I held him through the night.

We were off once again to the embassy the following morning. This time, Cory found swollen glands, could hear small crackles in Christian's lungs, and noticed that there was a rash developing at the base of his neck. He wasn't sure what it was. Christian's throat was more inflamed than the day before, and Cory decided to put him on antibiotics.

The third night was no easier for Christian. He showed no improvement. His temperature did not go below 102 despite regular aspirin. Cory wanted to do some blood tests on Christian and asked if I would assist him in the lab which I did. Christian's white blood count was sky high—indicating a virulent infection but Cory couldn't identify what was going on. He did not like what he was seeing.

There were only two commercial flights out of Guinea each week. On Tuesdays and Friday. It was now Wednesday, and Cory determined that if we did not see improvement for Christian in the next twenty-four hours—that he wanted Christian out on the Friday flight. It was an Air France flight from Conakry directly to Paris.

All departing diplomats had to obtain exit visas to leave Guinea. Once again it was a requirement which was against the Geneva Conventions, and it had caused embassy personnel delays on occasion. But there had never been a delay in a medical situation. Bill began the visa process for Christian and me the following morning so that we would be ready to go if it was necessary.

By late Thursday afternoon, Christian was not showing any improvement. We were trying to get as many liquids into him as possible to keep him from getting dehydrated. His temperature was not coming down, and he was increasingly lethargic. You could see on his face that he felt terrible. If he was not crying, he had a quiet whimper. He was developing an ear infection and was increasingly pulling at his ear. He now had a rash over much of his body which Cory still could not identify.

I had already started packing our things when Bill came to the house from the embassy. The Guinean government had not approved our exit visas. We were not going to be able to leave the following day for care for Christian.

A line now had been crossed that was way beyond the norm of irritating and psychological harassment. The wife of an American diplomat and their baby was being prevented from obtaining medical care. We were unofficially held hostage and our baby was being allowed to suffer.

The flight came and left on Friday, and we were not on board. Christian saw no improvement. It now was going to be Tuesday before we would be able to depart Guinea. And we still had no exit visa.

On Saturday afternoon, I would look up to see a most unusual sight. Walking down our driveway was the only Guinean physician in the country, one of only four Guinean college graduates in the country who was still alive. He was walking side by side with the doctor from the Russian embassy. The word had gone out in the community that Christian was sick, and in defiance of both Guinean law and the Russian Ambassador's edicts, the doctors had decided that they would come together to see if they might be of help.

It was a moment when one realizes the universal unifying nature of humanity when selfless concern takes precedent over the edicts and actions of extreme forces—no matter their origin. Unfortunately, their examinations offered no greater insight into what was happening with Christian. It was clear that we had to get to a medical center outside of the country.

We continued through the weekend doing everything we could for Christian. He was a very sick baby. Word came that the head of Air France, in Guinea, wanted to talk with us. He was well aware that we had been denied exit visas for the previous flight. He came to tell us that if the permits were denied again that he would attempt to board us through the cargo hold. His instructions were that we were to go to the airport on Tuesday, assuming that we would get our visas. If we did not receive approval to exit, he would nod for me to take Christian into the cargo area. He planned to box us up to take us through the cargo hold to get us out.

Christian had now been sick for over a week. He would show slight signs of improvement but only briefly. We had to get him out of the country. When we left for the airport, we still had not received our exit visas. Finally, in the last moments before we were to be 'crated' we received word that we would be allowed to leave.

It was Christian and me who were leaving. Will remained behind with his father.

We arrived at the American Hospital in Paris, late in the night. A car from the embassy in Paris and a nurse met us and took us directly there. Christian was immediately put on an IV, and a cot was brought into his room so that I could stay with him. By morning, first blood tests were returned and I was told that Christian had a gram-negative bacterial infection, which made it resistant to most standard antibiotics. It would only respond to a specific highly sophisticated antibiotic. Further, they said that he also had an unusual and serious virus. His ears were terribly infected, and the doctor recommended that they puncture his eardrum. I had no way of questioning the recommendations of the doctors. I gave my consent. It was horribly painful for Christian, and I could only pray that I had done the right thing.

Christian at 10 months old

Within a day or so Christian would slowly begin to improve. But it was slow. There seemed to be a steady stream of doctors and nurses coming to see this little towheaded American diplomat. He had an incredibly good disposition despite his illness. He won all of their hearts. He would remain in the hospital for a month. Except for excursions for a few minutes at a time, I stayed in the room with him throughout that time. Sometimes in the evening when he was asleep I would wander down to the courtyard in the hospital for a bit. But I had no desire to be away from him at all.

I disliked the fact that I had had to leave Will, who was just under three years old. It helped only slightly that I knew that his father was giving him enormous attention and paying attention to the details of his well-being. The embassy closed in the afternoon for lunch, so Bill was not out of the house for many hours at a time. I knew that the few wives in the embassy would be volunteering to spend time with Will as well. There was no way for me to have brought him with me. It did not go past me that it would have been questionable as to whether I would have returned to Guinea if he had been with me.

The day came when we were finally able to go back. Christian was back to his healthy self and received full medical clearance to return. There seemed to be no remnants of his illness.

By the time of our return, I had had a chance to contemplate what had happened and the awful fact that we had been denied departure. I assumed that it would be a huge topic of discussion between the US Department of State and Guinean officials. There was nothing about the harassment, confiscated mail, break-ins, and guns pointed at us that I found amusing in any way. I now looked to those who had brought us to Guinea, to take steps to make things right. It didn't happen.

Word soon came to the embassy from Washington. Secretary Henry Kissinger did not want us to make waves about what had occurred. It was not to be public knowledge. Watergate was in full swing. There was to be a complaint from the Ambassador at the local level, but there would be no other ramifications for the Guinean government that this had been allowed to happen.

At that point, my attention was solely on Will and Christian. I quietly simmered over what had taken place and the conditions under which we were living. But I stayed busy. I also found escape in meditation, and in writing and began to count down to our departure from Guinea.

I was thankful, and had an attitude of gratitude, that both Will and Christian had come through two critical episodes. First, Will, with the chimpanzee; and then Christian's illness. In both cases, it could have been a disaster. I gave thanks repeatedly that we were safe again. Except that we were not. Christian's illness had only begun.

Will and Christian

I was ready to be back in the States. After two tours in Africa, we were automatically assigned back to Washington. By that time, Watergate was just in the past. President Ford was in office

CHAPTER 14

Raison d'Etre

———◆———

AN OBVIOUS QUESTION—WHY WERE WE even in Guinea? Over the years we found that most people had no idea where Guinea was located. They often would confuse Guinea, in Africa, with New Guinea in the Pacific Islands. The reality was that this tiny country was of strategic importance to the US and other nations. Forty-percent of the world's bauxite, from which aluminum is made, is located in Guinea. Thus when Sekou Torre renounced Western influence, the Russians and Chinese took full advantage to set up contracts to mine the country. Before the departure of the French, Guinea was also known for its pineapple farms and had a relatively healthy local economy.

Alcoa Aluminum managed to get its foot in the door and was located in the northeast part of the country. The US remained to protect its small foothold and to keep tabs on main movements by the Russians and Chinese in the area. Guinea was also the training ground of the PLO, and some of those activities could be tracked as well.

Throughout our stay in Guinea, I was glad there was an American presence. We could represent our country well—even if only to a limited degree—and I felt that by being present—Guineans around us saw a positive side to America.

What often gets lost in stories about Africa, is the overall kindness and gentleness of so much of the population. Sekou Torre ruled with an iron fist. He drove people to keep their eyes down in hopes that they would not be noticed. But within the population were the majority of individuals who showed kindness towards their neighbors. It was a given that the smallest morsel of food or money would be shared with their families.

We saw many times when we might have helped our neighbors in Guinea. We dared not, however. We could not do so without placing them in danger. Unfortunately, we would also come to realize that our service to our country may also have cost our son his life.

CHAPTER 15
First Stop a Big Mac

———◆———

WILL, CHRISTIAN AND I WERE headed back to the States. Our two-year tour in Guinea was over. The State Department was having trouble getting a replacement for Bill, and he was asked to stay on for a few extra weeks. I would bring the kids back and look for a home to buy. When Bill and I left for Africa, we were newlyweds, living in an apartment. We were returning to the States as a family.

For two years we had been careful not to look strangers in the eyes less we get them in trouble. We had lived in a cocoon—somewhat denying events around us. We also had experienced a sense of helplessness when we could not get help for Christian.

I felt pure joy when we touched down at National Airport in Washington, D.C. Will was four, and Christian was two. At those ages, they were both troopers when it came to traveling. We had an overnight stop in Paris, and then a direct flight to Washington. About fourteen hours in flying time. It was before the advent of video games. The kids were content with coloring books and plastic figures for play. I always made sure I traveled with plenty of snacks in case of delay. They could sleep almost any place, but you cannot explain away hunger to small children. I made sure we always had some special treat that they would enjoy.

I rented a car and pulled out of the airport. One of the first sights were the golden arches. I had not had a Big Mac in about five years. I pulled in, and Will and Christian got their first introduction Mickey D's. As we walked through the door, a fresh-faced young woman smiled warmly and welcomed us. I burst into tears at being greeted by a stranger with a genuinely friendly face. It had not dawned on me how relieved I was to be back on American soil where being friendly is considered normal. We were home.

CHAPTER 16

Welcomed Home With Open Arms

AT THE TIME THAT WE left the United States, there were two of us. Now there was a wonderful family of four. We had put a few things in storage but basically we were starting from scratch to set up a household in the Washington, D.C. area. As there had been little in the way of outside entertainment, particularly during our last two years in Africa, we had diligently saved our money, to purchase a home when we returned to the States.

I was reaching the milestone thirtieth birthday. As a young adult of the 1960's, I had mildly scoffed at the getting married—have kids—buy a home—send the kids to the right schools—American dream. Now I was living the American dream. Further, women's lib was in full swing. That meant, so the tune went, we could have it all.

I had hoped, upon returning to the States, in 1974, that I would be able to find a part-time research or writing job. Prior to leaving Washington, I had been blessed by a progression of opportunities on Capitol Hill. I had started out as a research assistant to Republican Congressman John Dellenback, and had successively been promoted to press aide and then legislative aide. As his legislative aide, I then worked on a joint Congressional task force on several key pieces of legislation. Those were days when the words compromise and joint effort resounded positively within both the

Democratic and Republican parties. Vietnam was in full swing, and joint efforts did not take away the significance of policy differences.

I grew up in Florida, during the days when moderates were mostly Democrats. I then worked for Republican Nelson Rockefeller in New York, where Democrats seemed, at the time, mostly associated with strong union demands. Not much has changed in my fundamental views through the years. I define myself as a moderate who has worked for both parties. I support the balance between free markets and policies which address the needs of families, the need for access to good health care for all Americans, and policies which minimize prejudice, crime and the misuse of our freedoms.

Among so many things for which I am grateful is the role of mentors. I had the opportunity to work for several individuals who epitomized the best that America has to offer. One of those individuals was Esther Peterson. I was introduced to Esther while serving as a staffer for Republican John Dellenback. I was to represent moderate Republicans on a joint task force on Occupational Health and Safety. Esther represented the Democratic members. She was seventy-four, and I was twenty-four when we met. We hit it off immediately.

Esther was the first woman to be named an Assistant Secretary of Labor. She was a feminist long before there was such a term and before there was a popular movement. She fought for women's rights, fair pay, health care, day care and safe working environments. She would later be named President Kennedy's Consultant on Consumer Affairs, as well as to the same post under Presidents Johnson and Carter. She worked diligently to bring unit pricing to grocery stores so that shoppers could compare apples to apples. She was a consummate professional. She knew the ramifications of significant issues, and had the ability to bring people together for a common ground. We worked together for about nine months before I left the States. I greatly appreciated that she referred to me as a colleague, overlooking the fact that I had only a tiny percentage of her experience. I felt as though I learned something from her each day.

Bill and I had now been on tour for almost six years. I had loved the time I had spent as a stay at home mom. Christian was ready for nursery school, and Will was in his last year of kinder garden. I had written free-lance for magazines and newspapers while we were overseas. The best of all worlds, as far as I was concerned, was to go back to work part time. I wanted to be home when my children came home from school.

I had thought I would come back to the States, look for a new home, get the kids settled into school; and then think about where I might get a job. Things did not work out that way. A couple of days after having my feet on the ground in Washington, I called Esther to say hello. Much to my surprise, as soon as she heard my voice, she asked if I could be at her home the following afternoon to talk with her.

Will, Christian and I were in temporary quarters provided by the State Department. Bill was still in Guinea. There were mostly military wives and families where we were staying, in pretty much the same circumstances. Mostly their husbands were finishing tours or transitioning in some manner. Someone had already mentioned to me that there was a day care center just a few blocks away which was operated by the base. State Department families had access to it as well. I could leave Will and Christian there for a couple of hours while I went to visit Esther.

It felt great that I was being welcomed back to the States by someone who had been so kind to me and whom I respected so much. Esther had made it clear as soon as she heard my voice that she had something in mind. I had no idea what it was. Before leaving the States, my work with her had been part time. I thought perhaps there might be some similar opportunity.

It turned out that it was far greater than that and set a path that led to working with the Congress, the White House and senior posts over the next ten years in Washington.

Esther was now the consumer advocate for Giant Food Stores in the Washington, D.C. area. She had shepherded legislation through the Congress to require unit pricing in stores, and she was seen on TV regularly giving consumer tips. She looked like everyone's wise grandmother. Her silver-haired advice played well in the TV spots. She had a new endeavor in which she proposed that I become involved. She had just been named a Commissioner on a joint Presidential and Congressional Commission under President Ford. The purpose of the Commission was to evaluate Federal programs. Its mission was to make recommendations which would sustain the goals of various programs but reduce the regulatory and administrative burden of unnecessary requirements.

Esther Peterson – White House Consultant on Consumer Affairs - Presidents Kennedy, Johnson & Carter

Commissioners set policy and oversaw the direction of the Commission. Each Commissioner would have a personal staff representative on the Commission and there would be full-time staff investigating and making recommendations to take forward to the Congress and the White House. Esther wanted me to be her personal staff representative on the Commission. The Commission was composed of Congressmen, Senators, the Governor of Indiana, the Director of the US Office of Management and Budget, the Director of the IRS, and a diverse group of public interest representatives. It was a bipartisan Commission with representation from multiple major sectors.

No staff had yet been selected. The Commissioners had not even been sworn in. Esther explained that the bipartisan and high profile nature of the commission would put a good deal of pressure on staff members. She felt that I had proved myself as a capable and trustworthy individual. She wanted me to be her personal representative on the Commission. I was, of course, deeply honored that Esther would even consider me as her staff person.

This was a more demanding opportunity than I had considered. It also was an exciting opportunity. I was thrilled to have the possibility of coming back into the Washington environment in which I had thrived. It went way beyond the discussion that I would seek a part time position once we were settled and the kids were in school.

I had virtually no communication with Bill, as he was still in Guinea. He was due back in the States within a few weeks. Esther said that staffing would not get underway for several weeks. She wanted to start giving me background information so that I could fully understand the mission of the commission. She knew that I understood what was being offered. And she was giving me time to see if I might work it out.

I could not immediately make a decision. I realized that I would have to have a structure which would be supportive of the kids whether I was working part time or full time. I immediately began the search for a new home—looking at various homes in Washington, Arlington, and other areas surrounding Washington.

My starting point was that I wanted an area where there were lots of other children. They, too, had been somewhat isolated in Guinea. I wanted to be sure that we were in a community where there was plenty of opportunity for contact with other children and an environment where there were caring teachers.

It seemed over the next couple of weeks that the path was laid out for me. After looking in several areas, I began to explore Reston, Va., outside of Washington. It was a planned community with lots of play-grounds, walking and riding paths, and an excellent community school. The school even had a list of after school qualified sitters. I quickly began to rationalize that after serving my country overseas for six years, and giving most waking moments to taking care of Will and Christian, that I deserved this opportunity to restart my career.

I had not officially accepted Esther's offer before Bill returned. But I had been able to set up a structure which made the decision tenable. I did not have to do much convincing where Bill was concerned. He readily agreed that we would give it a try.

Bill had been an involved father from the beginning. There was no question that we would both continue to care enthusiastically for Will and Christian. Bill was in a position to leave work right on time and was the first to arrive home. He left before me in the morning, and I was able to arrange my schedule so that I would have breakfast with the kids and deliver them to school. They both thrived in their new environment. Our after school sitter was caring and loved to bring cookies and treats from home.

The Commission proved to be both a demanding and incredibly satisfying opportunity. I wound up writing the policy paper which laid out the essentials for fulfilling the goals of the Commission. By the time we finished our mission, I had been named Assistant Director of the Commission. Our recommendations were accepted by the Congress and the White House. There was consensus that we had strengthened programs and saved taxpayers several billion dollars. At every level, it was successful.

Will and Christian thrived. I felt incredible satisfaction from the challenges and the knowledge that I had met the expectations of Esther, and eventually, the other Commissioners, in completing the goals of the Commission. I received virtually daily praise and public acknowledgment for my efforts during the next four years. I felt a tremendous sense of camaraderie with my colleagues and loved being back on American soil.

They say, you can't go home again. In my case, I gratefully picked up where I had left off, and loved the time and place in which we were now living.

CHAPTER 17
A Weakness in the Armor

"Be strong in the Lord and in his mighty power...Put on the
full armor of God, so that when the day of evil comes,
you may stand your ground."

EPHESIANS 6:10-18

WHILE I WAS THRIVING — "WE" were not. Without even realizing it con-
sciously, Bill Wagner and I were walking down two different paths. While
I was enjoying our time back in the States, diplomats are not supposed to
be sitting behind a desk in Washington.

As time passed, the challenges of Africa did not fade for me. I
found that it did little good to talk about what had occurred. It seemed
that no amount of time would take away the sting of having held my
dear Christian, ten months old, hour after hour, while being refused by
a government to get medical care. At that time, America was blissfully
unaware of the developing dangers for American diplomats around the
world.

Even in Washington, there seemed to be little awareness of the
diminishing protection afforded by carrying a diplomatic passport. I
had been isolated for over two years, had nearly lost my baby, had had

my other son subjected to rabies shots. We had been aware of members of the Guinean population who disappeared in the night, never to be heard from again. I had gone through months of illness myself. The term post-traumatic stress syndrome did not exist.

I expressed my opinion, in 1974, upon returning to the States, that the lack of official response to our detention in Guinea, could contribute to a lessening of concern for the safety and well-being of diplomats in difficult posts. I felt that my concern was noted. And that was all that I felt that I could do.

Going public in situations involving our diplomats and foreign nationals with whom we worked overseas might mean putting people in danger and result in deaths. Eventually, several steps were taken within the State Department and by the Congress, to acknowledge what happened during our tour. It did not change what happened but it was good to know that our efforts were understood.

For the first two years back in the States, we didn't need to discuss the future. We had been in hardship posts for two tours, and it was policy for us to be back in the States for at least one tour. Thus, we weren't back because of a refusal on my part to remain overseas. We were, initially, back because it was US policy to have us back in the States.

However, after the first two years—it was time to consider where we would go next. Bill was willing to entertain virtually any post to which we might be assigned. It went without saying that my original thought that we would do a couple of tours and then take up life in the States permanently—was not going to be the reality. As I thrived in what I was doing in Washington—success for Bill was in service to the country overseas. In some respects, the more challenging the better.

I didn't have too much difficulty in bargaining with Bill to remain in the States for the four-year mission of the Presidential Commission.

It caused some concern for him, but he did not press to leave before the completion of my 'tour' stateside.

Several posts were suggested to us over the next couple of years. It became apparent from our discussions — that at the deepest level—I was not prepared to take the kids back into a blatantly anti-American situation. In fact, it was not until we were assigned to our next post, that I realized how difficult it was going to be for me to leave at all.

By the time the Commission on which I was working was winding down, my mentor, Esther Peterson, had been appointed as President Carter's Consultant on Consumer Affairs. She was now well into her late seventies. She was still as effective as ever, but she let me know that she was moving in the direction of retirement. Much to my surprise, I once again received a call from her, this time asking me to come to the White House.

Esther explained that she was getting close to retiring and that she would like to recommend me to replace her as the President's Consultant on Consumer Affairs. I was thirty-three years old, and that was a cabinet level post.

On the day that I was asked to go to the White House, Bill came home to tell me that we had received our new assignment—to Casablanca, Morocco.

Over the next period of weeks, we had many heartfelt discussions. We had gone through moments in previous years when we were not sure we would stay together. We had not sought counseling and we had not found direction in prayer together. I suggested from time to time that we seek a counselor but had met resistance. I, at the time, did not take the step of doing so on my own. Through our discussions, however, we seemed to be aligning our goals. I had had my four years back in the States. It was time to let Bill move forward with his career and his commitment to service to the country.

I would let Esther know that I needed to put my family first. I would thank her for even considering me as her nominee to President Carter.

Bill left first for Casablanca. I would stay in Washington, until June, to let Will finish school and to finish up my time on the Commission. That time proved to be harder than I anticipated. I now had to wind up things at work and be full time mom and dad to Will and Christian. I had to place the house on the market to be rented and do all of the packing of the household. Once again it would not be easy to substitute isolation for friends.

It proved to be a disaster. It took every effort in my being to step onto the plane to go to Morocco. Unlike our can-do team attitude starting out on our first adventure in Africa, we both took one step after another which quickly led to the end of our marriage.

Within months, I was back in the States. Our marriage had totally disintegrated. Remaining in Morocco, was no longer a choice. I agreed to allow Will and Christian to stay in Morocco, for a period of months, so that their father would not go a full tour without seeing the kids. At that point, however, there was no discussion of reconciliation.

I knew that divorce and temporary separation from the kids were going to be terribly painful and, upon returning to the States, virtually immediately got myself into professional counseling. As one does in a foxhole, I also put myself into the hands of the Lord. I regretted that, we, together, had not taken those two steps together, long before I wound up in that place alone.

While we would both subsequently make some effort to repair our marriage, the reality was—I was done with the foreign service. I did not want to injure Bill in his service to our country. I was not prepared, however, to spend a lifetime overseas, to move repeatedly, and to isolate myself and perhaps the kids, from the friends and family I loved dearly. I had never wanted to be an expatriate. It was clear that Bill was just beginning the career that he wanted. I respected the job that he was committed to do overseas. It was a life for him but not for me.

We quickly agreed we would work together to be as good parents as we could be. We wrote a joint commitment to that effect and to acknowledge our care for each other. But we would walk separate and different paths.

My separation from Will and Christian was as painful as I had imagined. I tried almost to create a cocoon for myself by moving into an efficiency apartment in Washington, where I would remain until just before the boys came back to me. I did not want to be in an empty house without them. I also never had lived by myself. There were few nights initially that I did not cry myself to sleep. I knew that I could not go back but the path to renewal and healing, would require a large amount of effort and focus on my part.

My apartment was back on Capitol Hill, where I could immediately submerge myself into the church I had attended so many years before. I went into counseling through the church. I became determined that I would get myself on the most stable track possible. When the kids came back to me, I wanted to be ready to focus on them. I wrote to them virtually every day and had a time set with Bill so that I could call Casablanca, to speak with them each week. In my heart, however, I knew the calls and letters did not replace my presence.

The Commission, on which I had worked for four years, had wound down. Once again, my mentor of so many years, Esther Peterson, offered me an opportunity. It allowed me to be productive but was low profile and far less demanding than the position I had been in for several years or at the level she had previously proposed.

A task force was forming in the White House, on Domestic Advisor Stuart Eizenstat's staff, to complete a White Paper for President Carter on the constitutional implications of certain laws related to privacy in financial and medical records. A two-year commission on privacy had just made a set of recommendations to the White House and Congress. The task force was to take those recommendations and consider their ramifications for government, individuals, business, and communications capability.

I shared an office in the Old Executive Office Building on the White House grounds and spent the next period of months working collectively with the other task force members and slowly putting my life on a stable path.

As so many others do, during the previous few years, when all seemed to be going well, going to church and my attention to prayer had diminished. Another layer of disagreement between Bill and myself had related to the church. He had turned away from organized religion during college, and he had not been receptive to my proposed involvement in the church.

In the future, I would look back at the difficulties our disagreements had caused and think about the path that we might have followed. We had two beautiful sons from our marriage. I could tell myself that we had done all that we could to care for them and assure them of our love. I could tell myself that we needed to follow different paths.

Deep down, however, I knew that our thought processes, left on their own, led us away from answers we might have found in counseling, prayer and a fuller understanding of the Word of the Lord. A writing on divorce given to me by my Christian counselor likened divorce to a great tree being divided by a bolt of lightning. Part of the tree might heal, but there would always be evident scars from the tearing apart of that which God had joined.

A year after our separation I felt that I had let God down. We had made a vow for better or worse and in sickness and health. We did not keep those promises. I had turned to the Lord while we were in Africa. But when we returned to the United States, I certainly had turned much of my attention to the excitement and challenges inside the Capital Beltway.

By leaving little time for reflection and prayer, and by turning solely to our intellectual capabilities to deal with our issues, we failed to allow the Lord's presence to be our guiding principal. One morning at church, a year after our divorce, my minister asked in passing how I was doing. I answered, "I am dealing with everyday life pretty well, but feel as though I let God down." He answered, "You did." He went on to say, "Being human can be a bitch sometimes. Right?"

None of us escapes the need for grace, forgiveness, and redemption in our lives. Whether it is for menial slip ups or shameful offenses, none of us escapes the reality of the price that Christ paid for our sins.

I would begin to understand actually why God's love for us could not be dependent on our success or good works. Simply put, none of us, no matter our good intentions, walks through life without sin. God did not intervene in the death of Christ for our greater good.

John 3:16 "For God so loved the world, that he gave his only begotten Son, that whosoever believes in him should not perish but have everlasting life."

Isaiah 53:12 "He bore the sin of many."

My separation for a period from the church and from paying attention to guidance from the Lord came with a price. As I drew back to the Lord, I would be grateful each day for His presence and direction. I came to have a fuller understanding of the sacrifice that Christ made for our forgiveness.

In the months following our marriage separation, I made a commitment to myself that I would do everything possible to get myself stabilized before the kids came back to the States.

During that time with the counselor, I was able to address the effects of having been molested, the stresses of the years overseas, and the loss of my marriage and separation from my children. The counselor went so far as to suggest that while he found that I was psychologically a stable person—that had I not returned to the States—that further isolation overseas would have been disastrous.

At no time had I considered hurting myself. However, I certainly agreed with the message, that at no point should I ever allow myself to turn inwardly and try to depend only on my own resources through life's most difficult times. It was not desirable nor necessary. In any circumstance, the Lord is present for us all.

**Psalm 34:18, "The Lord is near to the brokenhearted
And saves those who are crushed in Spirit"**

Just before the kids returned, I moved into a townhouse on Capitol Hill and found that the Capitol Hill Day School was an excellent school which had caring teachers and took advantage of the wealth of resources available at the various museums in Washington. The house was on a park and the kids could walk to school and home with me or their after school sitter. I once again found a caring after school sitter with whom the kids were happy.

Will and Christian entered school, quickly made friends, and became involved in after school soccer and other activities. Shortly after their return, I was recruited to become Special Assistant to the US Comptroller of the Currency, the regulator of National Banks. Once again I was in a demanding position. However, again I was able to set my schedule so that I had breakfast with the kids and my office was only a few minutes from home. I was able to go to soccer games and participate fully in their activities. Bill was serving in still another embassy in Africa.

CHAPTER 18

Getting Steady with Help From the Lord

———◆———

THERE WERE A SERIES OF significant events in the year that followed our divorce on February 13, 1979. Bill had come back to the states for a brief court appearance — which took place in the Judge's quarters.

We had a non-combative separation and divorce process. We even had the same attorney who appeared with both of us before the judge. My career had taken a path that gave me financial stability. There was only a matter of division of property, assurances that we would have joint custody, and steps to work out means so that the kids were both safe and were able to spend time with their father. It had only taken us a matter of minutes to decide on the division of our property and we had agreed to joint custody before seeing the attorney. While overseas Bill never faltered in his commitment to spend time with his sons.

Following court, I had taken a deep breath. I still had feelings for Bill. But as we left the courthouse he gave a high sign to the attorney. He seemed to be saying that he had gotten what he wanted in the divorce. I felt sad. However, I knew that the Lord was there for me, and I had done a great deal to pick myself up. I had become involved in the church that I loved, had resolved many internal issues in my life, and most importantly, had my children back in the States with me for the foreseeable future. I was ready to continue to move forward.

Not so fast.

One day after going to court, Bill took the kids to a movie. He would be leaving Washington in just a couple of days. I left my house, driving my small Fiat convertible, for a dinner party with friends. I drove two blocks and entered the intersection. I had the green light. As I entered the intersection, I saw a car to my left. It appeared to be stopping for the red light but suddenly the driver gunned the gas and crashed straight into my side of the car. My head hit the steel latch of the convertible, and I went down on the seat. The car spun around and for a moment I thought I would be hit again. I was hurt badly.

Cars pulled over to help, and the police were called. The police officer asked me what had occurred, and I explained that I had had the green light and that the woman had not stopped. He turned to her, expecting her to claim that she had the green light. Instead, she said that it was true that she had run the red light. The police officer looked incredulous when he asked her whether she had seen the light and why she had not stopped. She replied matter-of-factly, "Yes, I saw the light, I just didn't feel like stopping." She reaffirmed that statement two years later in deposition and never seemed to show any remorse for her actions or concern for my injuries. Later, my attorney would comment to me that he was a former prosecutor and that he had seen hardened criminals with greater remorse than she had shown.

I was taken by ambulance to the hospital, and the officer went to find Bill at the theater to let him know what had occurred. I was released a day later, and Bill returned to Africa.

Over the next period of months, it was clear that I had received a substantial injury. I had memory difficulties, developed seizures and lost a good deal of my hand-eye coordination.

I quickly figured out ways to deal particularly with the memory loss, namely writing down every conversation I had at work, to be sure that I would not miss anything. I had to carry a map with me in my car as I could no longer remember routes that I had traveled many times. As time passed, fortunately, the memory issues would abate. I wound up on anti-seizure medication, however, for almost six years, and had to undergo rather extensive physical therapy.

Once again my colleagues were empathetic and helpful. The Comptroller was satisfied that I would be able to keep up with my responsibilities and was also supportive.

Again, my children proved to have tremendous resilience. They were enjoying school, had good friends, liked life back in the States, and were happy. They seemed relatively un-phased by what had occurred. I struggled but kept complaints to a minimum. I did not want to give Bill any excuse for trying to convince me that the kids should go back with him. Thus, I had the incentive to become as healthy as possible as quickly as possible. I would continue to have physical effects from my injuries for years. However, I also was able to function very well. Later, I would learn that I could depend on the Lord for complete healing.

During 1979, I generally was focused internally on life. However, I grew up in a family that often met the call to look beyond themselves, to show concern and to take action. I would soon find that the Lord would give me a gift and an opportunity to serve in a most unusual way.

Towards the end of 1979, there was an event that our country would never forget. On November 4, 1979, the American Embassy in Tehran was overrun, and sixty-six Americans were taken hostage. We had served with one of the men, Charles Jones, in the Congo. He was dedicated to the foreign service and had a wonderful family. Our children had played together many times. As was true of most Americans, I was horrified by the unfolding events. At a personal level, my thoughts that American diplomats were coming under increasing difficulty and fire and that I needed to keep my children safe were re-enforced. I was grateful that they were with me.

All of America was heartsick for the hostages and their families. Most of us were glued to the television each night for news of what was occurring. Along with so many others, I prayed that they would feel the presence of the Lord with them.

I watched carefully when the hostages were paraded in front of the press. After a year in captivity, a toll had been taken, and the need to act on behalf of the detainees was obviously pressing.

As Special Assistant to the Comptroller, I was involved in security meetings and discussions regarding Iranian assets. I also was privy to increasing rumblings on Capitol Hill for the US to take aggressive action after a failed attempt to rescue the hostages. Many believed that there was no way that the hostages could now be freed in an attack. Many lives would be lost if we went down that path.

President Carter was being attacked relentlessly for what many perceived as weakness on his part for failing to order a major military rescue. The Iranians were masters at manipulating the press and events to turn the country's anger about the events on ourselves rather than the extremist regime.

It seemed to many that one of the goals of the Iranian regime was to affect the outcome of the next presidential election. They succeeded.

By now, it seemed the country was moving quickly towards a state of war with Iran. President Carter had lost the election — and there was no way that President Reagan and a hawkish Congress would let the situation continue through the following year.

That Thanksgiving, Will, and Christian were with their dad who was back in the States. I prayed for the hostages and found myself asking the Lord what might be done to prevent war and almost certain death for many of the hostages.

My prayers, for the first time in quite a while, were for others, rather than for myself or my children. Over that weekend, that still small voice began to speak to me.

CHAPTER 19

A Call from Within

———

"Call upon Me in the day of trouble; I shall
rescue you, and you will honor Me."

PSALM 50:15

THROUGH THANKSGIVING I FOUND MYSELF focused on what was happening
on Capitol Hill and the scenes of the hostages.   My internal dialog was
that something needed to be done that would let them and the world know
how much America supported them.   As the next couple of days passed, a
seed for an effort to support and pray for the hostages began to develop.

No matter what I did my thoughts kept coming back to that thought.
What about a day of national prayer to send a message of support to the
hostages and to seek peaceful resolution? My thoughts vacillated. Was I
being urged to take action or was my consternation a result of my identification with the events and knowing one of the prisoners?

By Saturday morning after Thanksgiving, I thought of my neighbor
who had been a missionary and who was an international negotiator.   I
decided I would talk with him.   I was sure that he would pat me on the
head and tell me to continue my prayers.   After all, why would the Lord
call me to this type of action? I was the person who had, in certain ways,

in the previous several years turned away from the Lord, had broken my marriage vows, and was struggling to find my way through the future. It was true that I was once again a participant in my church, and I prayed sincerely for the Lord's healing and direction. I was not, however, a church leader nor charged in any way theologically to provide any public leadership.

Despite that, I marched myself down to my neighbor's the following morning. He invited me in, and I explained my thoughts. At most, I thought that he might pick up the lead and perhaps work with others to organize a day of significance. After we had talked for a few minutes, he disappeared upstairs for a telephone conversation. When he came back down, he said that he thought I should call my minister at my church. He was encouraging, saying he would be happy to work with me after I had talked with my minister. I thanked him and returned home.

Shortly after that, I picked up the phone to call my minister. I called the church expecting to get a recording and to leave a message that I would like to talk with my minister. Much to my surprise, our minister, the Reverend James Adams, known simply as Jim by the congregation, answered the phone himself. I said that I had had a discussion with my neighbor who had encouraged me to call him. I told him that I was not sure where I was going with all of this and was looking for direction from him.

Much to my surprise, Jim asked me to come over to the church. We sat and talked. I told him of my concerns for the safety of the hostages, my belief in the power of prayer and that I felt that something needed to be done to try to foster a peaceful resolution rather than an attack to try to release the hostages.

Jim's response was that he felt I should stand up at church the following morning and explain my thoughts and concerns and to see how the congregation would respond.

Wow! Something like this had not been on my agenda forty-eight hours before. Since I had initiated the call to Jim, I obviously had to move forward to see how things developed.

For the first time in my life, I stood up publicly in church the next morning to state that I believe in the power of prayer, that I believed we needed to come together in prayer as a nation to support the hostages, and asked the congregation what they thought. The response was over-whelming. A large group of people encouraged me to think through what I was proposing and to continue to move forward. As it turned out, the head of the National Council of Churches was attending the church that weekend. He came up to me following the service, gave me his card and said he would like to work with me. He would be happy to send messages throughout the country to churches of all denominations calling for a day of prayer. Again, WOW! I could feel that something way beyond myself was underway. I had only to listen and to be willing to move forward.

Our rector then also suggested that I go back to my neighbor to discuss a plan. I returned home after church and once again presented myself to my neighbor. I told him what had occurred, and he responded that he had also made some calls. In fact, he had talked with Billy Graham and several other well-known national church leaders and that they were all prepared to take whatever action I wanted.

He put the matter directly and squarely in my lap. Looking me straight in the eye, he said, "Susan, you have answered a call from the Lord. I believe you are being moved by the Holy Spirit. We are here to support you."

It seemed that each time I sat down—the next step became clear.

I spoke almost immediately with Louisa Kennedy, spokesperson for the families of the hostages throughout the months. Her husband, Moorhead Kennedy, was the senior Economic and Commercial Officer of the Embassy and one of the detainees. She and the the families had established FLAG—the Family Liaison Action Group and worked tirelessly to keep lines of communication open and to do anything that might be supportive of their family members.

I explained to Louisa what I had in mind and that I had just begun to make calls and to move forward. Without hesitation, Louisa responded that the families would be appreciative of my efforts. We talked several times over the next several days and jointly chose the date of January 29, 1981, for the National Day of Prayer.

Over the next days, the effort took on a life of its own. It seemed from all directions — I almost just had to think about a step, and it would happen. I spoke with the Archbishop of the Roman Catholic Diocese of Washington, who then suggested that I contact the Washington Interfaith Conference. Within days, representatives of the Jewish, American Muslim, Protestant and Roman Catholic faiths had come forward. For the first time, an official of the American Muslim faith stepped forward publicly to call for the release of the hostages.

I enlisted the help of the press officer of the Office of the Comptroller, and we sat and constructed a plan to bring cohesiveness to the days ahead. At each turn, anyone who became aware of what we were doing wanted to participate and had constructive suggestions.

On December 8, 1980, a press conference was held at the Washington National Press Club to announce that there would be a National Day of Prayer to honor the hostages. Overnight, however, Louisa and I agreed to make a change in the purpose of the Day. Louisa and I explained to the gathered press corps, as well as representatives of multiple faiths, that while we wanted to get a message of support to the Hostages, that we were praying that the day would be a Day of Thanksgiving for the Return of the Hostages. At that point, there was no indication that a release was imminent.

From that day forward, all explanations included the prayer that January 29, 1981, would be a Day of Thanksgiving for the return of the hostages.

Within a day or so, I was able to pick up the phone and call Ward Grant, Bob Hope's publicist in Los Angeles and explain what we were doing. Years before, I had worked for an agent in NY, as a summer intern. I called that office to ask if they had suggestions for how I might reach Bob Hope to ask if he would do a radio spot for national distribution. That was at 6 in the evening Eastern time. The secretary in the agent's office didn't seem even to take a breath. Without hesitation, she said, "Here is Ward Grant's number in California. Call him. He will help you."

Sure enough, Ward Grant answered the phone himself, and without hesitation, instructed me to write a spot for Bob Hope and to fax it to him. Within two days, he had sent out tapes all over the country to be played on local radio stations.

One of the people with whom I had worked on the Presidential Commission was on the staff of the Governor of Indiana. I called and explained what we were doing. He immediately responded, "We will organize a proclamation to send to every governor in the country."

Shortly after that, my neighbor called to say that Pat Boone had done a radio spot. I had been clear with the press that I did not want my name in articles explaining the effort. I wanted this effort to be about the hostages — not about me. The press had respected that. My neighbor said that Pat Boone had done a special song specifically for me. That he had been told of my efforts privately and that he had wanted me to have a special message. I still have that tape today.

About two weeks into my efforts, I became concerned that I make sure that we were not doing anything that would hurt the efforts and negotiations that were taking place for the release of the hostages. I did not want a misstep on my part to cause unintended problems. At that point, I called the Iranian desk at the US State Department to be sure I was not causing difficulty. After a brief conversation, the State Department Officer responded to my concern: "I don't know everything you are doing, but whatever you are doing — keep on doing it." There was a measured excitement in his voice. I prayed that night that what I thought I had heard was real. Having been assured that my steps were positive, I knew to make no comment to anyone about what I felt I heard in the officer's voice.

What I was able to say to Louisa was that the officer had confirmed to me that word was already getting through to Iran that a massive effort of support for the hostages was underway.

An office had been set up in Washington, for the Families Liaison Action Group, the group formed by families of the hostages. Over the months, thousands of letters, drawings, quilts, and messages had been sent to that office for the families and for the hostages to see when they returned. Over the next couple of weeks, I spent a number of hours at the office helping to field phone inquiries and to help sort gifts which were pouring into the office over the Christmas holidays. There was, in that office, an aura of love. I had never experienced the overwhelming emanation of love which seemed to come off of the walls and from the cubbies of gifts. I hoped that all of the hostages would eventually see the array of greetings and care meant for them.

The next few weeks passed with many requests and follow-through from all over the country. I began to work with members of my church on the service that we wished to have on January 29th.

On January 20th, 1981, President Reagan took the oath of office. Within minutes, word came that the hostages were being released.

On January 22nd, Senator Mark Hatfield introduced S. Res. 16 - A Joint Resolution of Congress designating January 29, 1981, as "A Day of Thanksgiving to Honor Our Safely Returned Hostages". He had his staff call his fellow members of Congress, to ask them to join in the Resolution so that it could be presented as the President's first act of business. I worked with the Parliamentarian of the House and with the Legislative Office of the Library of Congress to draft the resolution and walk the necessary sign-offs through the Speaker's Office so that there could be a simultaneous vote in both the House and the Senate.

On January 23rd, the Resolution passed. It was presented to the President. There was a morning of some consternation as new White House staff weren't quite sure what was in order with the Resolution. Once again I was bumped along the chain until I was speaking directly with James Brady, the President's Press Officer. I explained to him what had occurred over the previous several weeks. I was well aware that the Resolution would become Public Law No. 1 of the new Congress if the President signed the Resolution into law immediately.

Several hours later I received a call from a staffer in James Brady's office saying that the President would sign Public Law No 1.

Following were President Reagan's remarks at the signing of the law: The President: "Good morning. The resolution before me, here on the desk, is the proclamation of thanksgiving, a joint resolution from the Senate and the House, already signed by the Speaker and by the Vice President, as President of the Senate. I am going to affix my signature to it, also, to simply take advantage of this opportunity to share in it. [At this point, the President signed the joint resolution into law.] This resolution pays tribute to the strength of America. It recognizes the principle of public service, which 53 men and women fulfilled in the highest tradition of their calling. It recognizes the devotion and bravery of professional soldiers, the memories of those eight men and the long line of those who have given everything to preserve everything. It reminds us that "greater glory hath no man than that he lay down his life for another." It salutes the unity of the nation when we're confronted with threats to our freedom. And finally, it expresses what we must all remember, that God watched over His servants during this difficult time of testing. I call on, as this resolution does, all Americans to join this Thursday in raising thanks that our sons and daughters have returned. They have shown by their example that the spirit of our country can never be broken." Note: The President spoke at 10:18 a.m. to reporters assembled in the Oval Office at the White House. As enacted, SJ. Res. 16, proclaiming "A Day of Thanksgiving To Honor Our Safely Returned Hostages," is Public Law 97-1, approved January 26. Citation: Ronald Reagan: "Remarks on Signing a Resolution Proclaiming a Day of Thanksgiving for the Freed American Hostages," January 26, 1981. Online by Gerhard Peters and John T. Woolley, The American Presidency Project. http://www.presidency.ucsb.edu/ws/?pid=43835.

Following is an excerpt from the story written by the United Press International about what occurred on January 29, 1981. The headline read:

"Millions of Children Were Liberated from their Classrooms"

"Prayers of thanks were offered at church services across the nation in a National Day of Thanksgiving for the safe return of the 52 freed hostages. American people from all walks of life, of all colors, standing side by side, welcoming Americans home. In Washington, more than 150 anti-Khomeini Iranians demonstrated in front of the White House to honor the returnees. Indiana legislators paused from their work to join in a chorus of 'America the Beautiful.'

Cardinal Terence Cook celebrated a mass of thanksgiving at St. Patrick's Cathedral at noon Thursday, and Mayor Edward Koch was among those attending. Church bells pealed across Illinois at noon Thursday in honor of the hostages.

In Washington, leaders of four faiths led dozens of congressional employees and several House and Senate members
in a prayer service for the former hostages on the steps of the
Capitol. The brief noon service was one of thousands conducted across the nation.

'Many were the days when I said to God, I can't do it by
myself, I need You,' now returnee, Air Force Col. Tomas
Schaefer told a hushed congregation of about 2,000 who attended the interfaith service."

Millions gave thanks to God on that day that we were a United States of
America, that God had answered our prayers, and that the hostages were
safe. I also thanked the Lord for that still small voice over Thanksgiving,
which had turned into a phenomenal gift of service and grace. I had received a gift of the Spirit. I felt that Christian, who fought for his life as a
baby, was honored as well.

CHAPTER 20
Healing from Within

———————

IN THE YEAR FOLLOWING MY accident, in 1979, tests showed that I had developed scar tissue in my brain. I was having many hundreds of petit mal seizures. At times, sitting in a meeting, I would incur a confused look on the part of people in the room. I was, in fact, having moments of unconsciousness, without realizing it, and losing track of conversations. At times, I would answer a question without realizing that the conversation had moved on to a different subject.

Since MRI's were not readily available in 1979, eventually the neurologist called for an electroencephalogram which proved to be drastically abnormal. The way the neurologist described it to me was, "on a scale of 1 to 10 abnormality you are a 9". He did not expect that there would be an improvement with time. He prescribed an anti-seizure medication, Dilantin, for me.

The periods when I lost track of conversations disappeared. However, from time to time I would go for an EEG, and there was never much improvement.

I still found that under stress, I would get into the wrong 'file' in my brain and, at times, have a funny conversation with someone, when I replaced an intended word with a word which made no sense at all.

In a rush one morning, I stood at a hotel desk in NY, and explained to a clerk that I had moved my 'furniture' out of my room and would be back for it later. The clerk simply looked at me and said, "Yes, madam. That will be fine." It was a lot easier to return to the hotel to pick up my baggage rather than the furniture from the room in which I had stayed. Another time, I called out to a group already on an elevator to "please hold the elephant". That was embarrassing, as I then had to ride down with the people who had gotten what I had said but weren't sure that my personal elevator went to the top.

Over the next period of years, I meditated often. As had occurred in Africa, I found that mediation went a long way to help me deal with the stresses of my accident, dealing with life basically as a single mother, since my children's father was overseas, and a continued challenging and satisfying career. Beyond prayer and involvement in church, meditation brought me into presence with the Lord. I learned that silence in the presence of the Lord allowed me to be receptive to service and guidance rather than always being in the position of making a request. Just being present permeated all levels of my life.

Slowly, I began to visualize Jesus in my living room. He was sitting by the brick fireplace and I was sitting at His knee. In my mind's eye, I could see the Lord washing my brain. Theses meditations gave me a sense of safety and healing. I didn't like being on a medication if it was not necessary. I did not feel any particular side effects from the Dilantin. However, slowly, over a period of months, I began to reduce the amount that I was taking.

During that time, my neurologist continued to do EEG's. There was no sign of improvement. He was aware that I was gradually reducing the Dilantin. I was showing no signs of seizures. He was not thrilled that I was reducing my medication. The day came, however, when he said, "Look, Susan, you are not taking enough Dilantin to prevent seizures. If you have made up your mind that this is the road you want to go down, you might as well stop taking it. You are wasting your money." That was over thirty years ago.

I am not suggesting that one should refuse medical care in any way. I believe that most doctors are 'called' to their profession and bring their skill, and God inspired gifts to prescribe for their patients. I felt at my core, however, that I was healing from within. I felt safe in my decision. The EEGs did not improve. In other words, I was not cured. However, there has been no evidence that I have had seizures in the intervening thirty years. I believe that it was because, through prayer, meditation and visualization, that I was healed in body, mind and spirit.

I have found over the years, that I have been able to use the gift of prayer, meditation, and visualization, to assist others, both in seeking safety in the Lord and in assisting in healing. It has been a gift of sharing. I have been with friends dealing with terminal illness, and through the opportunity to share about the Lord, they have known that they were in the healing hands of the Lord. It has not been for me to determine in any way, the outcome of their illness, nor to deter them in any way from following their doctors' instructions but rather a gift to help them see, that no matter what, they were in the Lord's hands.

Exodus 25:8 "Let them construct a sanctuary for Me, that I may dwell among them."

I believe that we are all called and given the grace to create a safe haven, that He may dwell among us. We are given the choice to hear that call and to be open to it. Gifts of grace, loving kindness and healing are there to permeate our world.

CHAPTER 21
Nanoseconds in History

———

"Each one should use whatever gift he has
received to serve others, faithfully administering
God's grace in its various forms."

1 PETER 4:18

THERE HAVE BEEN PERIODS THROUGHOUT my life when I have been present
during what I understood, at the time, were significant events for America,
and, in some cases, the rest of the world. In general, my role was minute and
only momentary. In the scheme of things, my participation amounts to less
than a nanosecond in history. However, each of these moments of involvement served to reinforce in me, that as an individual and as an American, I
have the obligation to respect truth, to stand up for my beliefs, to appreciate
diverse points of view, and to put professionalism and responsibility ahead of
personal gain. At the end of the day, however, none of these events would
be of value at all, if in the process of observing or living them, I had failed to
understand, first, that each opportunity to serve is a gift.

The early 1980's saw three events which were in marked contrast to
each other. The first demonstrated the damage we do to ourselves and
others when greed becomes our idol, or put another way when there is
no internal compass. Many would go a step farther, and say, when left
to our own devices we lose our way. In the other two instances, for me,

132

the takeaway was to observe how much God's comfort was brought to the people who were involved, through our common love. And to wonder, once again, whether any of the individuals heard that still small voice.

On March 27, 1980, word came into the Office of the Comptroller of the Currency that the Hunt Brothers, Texas billionaire beneficiaries of the H.L. Hunt oil fortune, had failed to meet a margin call on silver futures contracts. The silver markets were plummeting. Margin is the amount of money which must be deposited when buying futures commodities contracts on an exchange.

At that time, I was serving as Special Assistant to the US Comptroller of the Currency. The Hunt brothers, Lamar and Herbert, had accumulated massive amounts of physical silver, and it had become clear that they were attempting to corner the world market. They held over 100 million troy ounces of silver. It was estimated that in less than a year, through manipulation of the markets, the brothers had profited by between $2 billion and $4 billion. The brothers had pyramided their holdings and paper profits through massive borrowing from major banks and securities firms.

Regulators, exchanges, and banks were all taking action to force the Hunts to cease their efforts. Since the Hunts were building their fortunes through using their paper profits as collateral for loans to purchase silver, the exchanges and the regulators began to raise the amount of actual cash that the Hunts had to deposit as margin for their purchases. If a margin call was missed, it meant the account owner's physical commodity would then be sold. Thus, when the brothers missed their margin calls, enormous amounts of Hunts' silver were instantly sold by brokerage houses so that adequate cash would be in their accounts. As prices plummeted, and margin calls were missed, silver was immediately sold, generating a further downward spiral.

At that time bank interest rates were at an all-time high, at around 17%. An inter-agency task force had been formed some months before to identify potential difficulties which might be created by the then overheated economy. As one of the only women on the task force, at age thirty-five, I was almost patted on the head by the older men, when some months before the crash, I had said that I thought that there would be a disruption in the commodity markets. Patronizingly, I was assigned to monitor the commodity markets from a banking point of view. I spent hours on the phone with exchange representatives, almost daily, gathering facts on what might be of significance each day. My efforts to establish relationships with exchange executives paid off. As the day passed, on what became known as Silver Market Thursday, I was able to get immediate information on what was occurring and the ramifications for banks and securities firms which were involved. Deputy Comptrollers were immediately scouring the major banks who had provided credit to the Hunt brothers or who had significant outstanding silver positions to determine the market and banking impact of the plummeting prices.

At approximately 6 P.M., I was sent, along with the Deputy Comptroller for International Banking, to the office of the Federal Reserve Chairman Paul Volcker, to brief him on what had occurred and the known impact on various banks. We left the Chairman's office at about 1 a.m. Billy Wood, the Deputy Comptroller for International Banking, turned to me and said, "Do you realize that the Chairman of the Federal Reserve just asked your advice about whether to let the markets open tomorrow?" I replied, "Yes, and the scary part is that I answered him." I recommended that the commodity exchanges be allowed to open.

The following morning, the Comptroller sent notes around to the Deputy Comptrollers which simply said, "She told you so."

The price of silver fell from over $50 an ounce to $4 an ounce in a matter of days. Fortunately, the markets stabilized, but many entities were left in shambles with the price remaining below $10. I would be part of the investigative team for Treasury to track exactly what had occurred and the breach by banks who had ignored regulators' instructions to forego further loans to the Hunt brothers. The inter-agency task force would make recommendations to the oversight agencies and the Congress to prevent in the future, the pyramiding of trading positions and paper profits, which had allowed the debacle to take place. This series of events altered my career and, much of my life, as eventually, I was appointed by President Reagan as Executive Director of the Commodities Futures Trading Commission, the actual regulator of the commodities exchanges. And, ultimately, I would leave government altogether to design and patent the first entirely computerized futures trading exchange system.

**Testifying before House of Representatives
Government Operations Committee**

March 30, 1981, a day of significance for all of America and the rest of the world. I was still serving as Special Assistant to the US Comptroller of the Currency. Word came early in the afternoon that an assassination attempt had been made against President Reagan. We suffered the same confusion as the rest of America, as first reports came that the President had not been shot, followed by confirmation that a bullet had come dangerously close to his heart.

The moment word came in that there was an attempt on the President's life, all key agencies went into lockdown, and emergency powers were declared. For our office, it meant that the banking agencies had to be ready to take whatever regulatory action was necessary, on a moment's notice, to deal with any attack upon the country. As part of the senior staff, we were immediately in mode, with extra security, to deal with what was happening. It was a long night for America and the rest of the world, waiting for news that the President would recover. While Secretary Haig caused some consternation when he stepped forward to declare himself in charge, until Vice President Bush returned to Washington, the fact was, that the best of American government, at many different levels, was working in a non-partisan and cooperative effort. In whatever area, for which they had a responsibility, staffers were on full alert, seeing to it that all measures were taken to deal with whatever event was occurring.

A few months later, on January 13, 1982, Washington and America was rocked with an event with a tragic outcome. Air Florida Flight 90 crashed into the 14th Street Bridge in Washington. It was a day that snow was blanketing Washington, and bringing everything to a halt. I was, at that point, Executive Director of the Commodities Futures Trading Commission, the senior staff person on the commission. At about 11:00 a. m., my long term friend, Terry Klasky, a lobbyist with the American Bankers Association, had called my office to invite me to a dinner with his fiancée. When I had been so badly injured in my automobile accident in 1979, Terry and his fiancée had, over a period of months, offered to take me grocery shopping, run my sons around when I could not drive, and had encouraged me through months of physiotherapy. Terry told me that he was about to go to Ft. Lauderdale for a meeting. It had already started to snow heavily, and I asked him if he was sure he wanted to fly out of Washington. He said he had to go. He had possession of some papers that had to be delivered. We talked for a few minutes and hung up. About ten minutes later I called Terry back. I believe it was that tiny voice of the Holy Spirit, urging me to make that call. I asked him once again whether he was sure that he wanted to try to take off out of Washington. He said yes. We talked for only a few minutes. I had had my say. It obviously was his decision.

In the next several hours my attention turned to what needed to be done in the agency before letting people leave early to deal with the heavy snowfall. As the senior staff person, it was up to me to be the last one out of the building and to be sure that necessary transfers of duties had been made to teams in other locations. The CFTC offices were located on 21st Street in downtown Washington. About the time that I was about to leave there were suddenly sirens and alarms everywhere. My car was the last out of the underground garage, and it would take me almost two hours to arrive home—just four miles away—with the 14th Street bridge between me and my home on 3rd Street. There were no cell phones so it would be almost an hour of sitting in the car before the news would come on the radio that a plane had crashed into the bridge.

Several hours later I sat before the television as everyone else did and it registered on me that Terry was probably on that flight. By morning, it would be confirmed to me that he had boarded the plane. He was sitting at the front of the aircraft and was killed instantly.

Approximately two weeks later a memorial was held for Terry at the House Banking Committee. His fiancée asked if I would do a eulogy for him. I could only thank him for his friendship, tell his family of conversations where he expressed so much love for them, and voice respect for his professionalism over the years within the banking community. Following the ceremony, several of us got into a conversation. It turned out that at least three of us had called Terry on the morning of the crash to express concern about his taking the flight.   I was reminded of the day, at twelve years old, that I had climbed into the car of my father's business partner, not knowing what my sense of danger meant. We all wondered whether Terry had heard that still small voice before boarding the plane.

CHAPTER 22
The Unthinkable

**"It is unthinkable that God would do wrong,
that the Almighty would pervert justice."**

JOB 34:12

SEPTEMBER 11, 2001. I AM dressing for a prayer breakfast in New Smyrna Beach, Fl. when the phone rings. Normally, the morning news would be on the TV, but I am running late. My phone rings, and it is Carol, my best friend from five years old. She asks if I have seen what is going on. I turn on the TV to see smoke coming out of the World Trade Center. Within a couple of minutes, a second plane flies into the South Tower. It was a tragic and horrifying morning for all Americans.

So many were affected that day. And for many, there will never be a complete recovery.

I had been sitting in the offices of Cantor Fitzgerald/ESpeed, in the World Trade Center, just two weeks before. Upon leaving the government, in 1982, I designed and patented the first totally computerized trading exchange system. In late 2000, E-Speed bought my patent and was in the midst of massive suits against five exchanges for patent infringement. As the inventor, it was up to me to defend my patent. I sat in the spot that no longer existed, and tragically, sat with several people who now were gone.

The story of my patent and the impact of the technology is one which went on for many years. The patent, itself, would play a role in the aftermath of September 11th. Initially, the technology was considered disruptive. It changed the trading of the US commodity exchanges from voice driven floor markets to computer-driven markets. In the process of bringing the technology to market, I had encountered all of the hurdles young entrepreneurs often face. It was a new technology which would enable some to make many millions of dollars, and cause others to lose their, sometimes illegal, advantage in the market. My system was designed to provide for first come first serve trading rather than giving the advantage to those who were direct participants on the floors of exchanges. Some of the largest corporations in America had become embroiled in the battle. And at times, I had found myself harassed and repeatedly the target of efforts to discredit both my invention and even to try to discredit me personally. Several corporations had pledged to bury me.

That still small voice once again served me well. At one point I had taken my core documents to my attorney and asked him to protect them. There had been several efforts to break into both my office and my home, and I was pretty sure that the target was the documents which substantiated my development of the patent. My attorney took those core documents, took up the area rug under his desk, placed them under the carpet, and put his massive desk back in place.

Within a week, my office was raided and thousands of pages of my documents, remaining at my office, disappeared. That was in 1984. All who might have had access, or who had reason to see the documents go, claimed that they had no knowledge of the location of the evidence. Repeatedly, over almost a twenty-year period, I testified regarding my background and the steps I had taken to develop the technology. Obviously, I was at a huge disadvantage without my papers. The good news was that the steps were etched in my brain, and I consistently stood by my testimony through years of depositions.

Many buildings in the Wall Street area were damaged as a result of 9/1l. The clean-up extended over many blocks. Within three months of 9/11, an unexpected discovery was made. Over ten thousand pages of documents proving my inventorship, which had been taken in 1984, turned up in the basement of a Wall Street building damaged by the attack. It was as though God, in the midst of this horrible tragedy, had handed the documents over to Cantor Fitzgerald/E-Speed for the good of the families of 9/11.

Over the period of months after 9/11, the legal battle over my patent, which had raged in the courts for years, softened. It seemed for everyone concerned, that a mutual solution, and respect for the impact and significance of the terrible loss of life, needed to be the real goal and outcome of the suits.

Eventually, E-Speed would settle the patent suits for over $50 million. Much of that settlement would go to be of assistance to the more than six hundred families of those who were killed on floors 100 to 104 of the North Tower.

The loss of my documents for so long, and pressures as a young single mother, to protect my children and to spare all of us from severe economic pressures, meant that I earned only a tiny percentage of the many millions made by others, as a result of my efforts. My view of that is that as always, God's good comes to all things, and it is gratifying to me, that my efforts resulted, in at least a small way, in helping to support the families of the victims of 9/11.

Today, we are all aware that there are millions who have suffered tragedies similar to the families of 9/11, and are refugees left virtually without support. I pray that each day, for those traveling this path, that they receive comfort rather than hatred. And that we, as Americans, and as part of the fellowship of humanity worldwide, may be instruments of God's love and direction.

Matthew 25:35-40 "For I was hungry and you gave me food, I was thirsty and you gave me drink, I was a stranger and you welcomed me, I was naked and you clothed me, I was sick and you visited me, I was in prison and you came to me... 'Truly, I say to you, as you did it to one of the least of these my brothers, you did it to me'

CHAPTER 23
For Those Who Walked Before

"I thank my God every time I remember you."

PHILIPPIANS 1:3

WHILE I HAVE HAD TO deal with physical challenges throughout my life, I have been blessed with overall good health.

In 1957, at age 57, my maternal grandmother was diagnosed with breast cancer. At that time the options for the treatment of cancer were relatively limited. It was determined that it was necessary to do a radical mastectomy, including the removal of her lymph glands under her arm. I do not recall whether there was follow-up radiation or chemotherapy. At the time, at age 12, however, I do remember the sense of danger and fear that went throughout the whole family. My best friend's grandmother had died recently after months of radiation treatment. The family knew that the fact that the cancer had reached my grandmother's lymph glands was threatening.

My grandmother did not hesitate to go ahead with a radical mastectomy. At that time there was no such thing as reconstruction. That meant that she used a prosthesis implant under her clothes. She had to deal with the trauma of losing her breast and the severe scarring across her chest and under her arms. The surgery also resulted in the chronic accumulation of fluid in her arm throughout the rest of her life. All of us took turns massaging her arm for twenty or thirty minutes at a time to relieve the discomfort.

Having said that, Riva Read Hemphill, my remarkable grandmother, lived to age 94. She loved the Lord, and she remained active throughout her life. She was interested in the world and lives around her until the day she died. I am grateful to have had a close relationship with her.

My grandmother lost her first daughter, Adley Dina Hemphill, at age six, in 1926. She had become suddenly ill, from a flu-like illness, and died in a matter of weeks. My grandmother, who was just thirty at the time, would go through periods of grief throughout her life.

Then the inconceivable occurred. Jane Hemphill Nelson, her daughter (my beloved aunt) who was born after Dina died, was diagnosed, in her late thirties, with breast cancer. She would follow a different path than my grandmother. It was thought that she was diagnosed at an early stage of her disease. Doctors recommended that she have a lumpectomy, along with the removal of several lymph nodes under her arm. She also received chemotherapy.

From the time that she was diagnosed until her death, at age forty-three, Jane enjoyed little peace and recovery from her cancer. She did not recover well from the surgery itself. It was necessary for her to have repeated surgeries over the next period of years, including skin grafts, to try to repair and help her incisions heal. Each surgery was debilitating. She would never be able to raise her arm fully again. The chemotherapy also made her terribly ill. This vibrant young woman would never regain her health. She had three young children, and the effects of her illness and her early death, would be traumatic and life changing for them.

Within a couple of years of her original surgery, it was determined that her breast cancer had metastasized into her liver. She fought a heroic but losing battle.

Apparently, the family bloodline for cancer had been established. Much to everyone's dismay, my mother's older sister, Riva Lief Erikson, was diagnosed approximately fifteen years later with breast cancer. Again, she would fight a valiant battle over the next years, but that insidious disease would metastasize to her colon. In 1990, she would be in Doctor's Hospital in Coral Gables, Florida, recovering from surgery, and my grandmother would lay dying, on another floor of Doctor's Hospital. When it was determined that my aunt had metastasized cancer, I had thought to myself that I did not see my grandmother surviving the death of a third child. It was too much to ask of her. After a relatively minor surgery, my grandmother went peacefully to the Lord, at age 94, with much of the family around her. She did not live to grieve the loss of a third child. Seven months later my treasured aunt, went to the Lord as well. My mother was the last of the siblings to survive, and she did not contract cancer.

There were six female cousins, including me, in the generation after my mother and my aunts. We all understood the potential ramifications of three close maternal family members with a history of breast cancer. We all began to have mammograms at early ages and diligently read and kept track of research and developments in the treatment of cancer.

One of my cousins who had lost her mother at too young an age, developed a somewhat fatalistic attitude toward potential outcomes if she too developed cancer. There was no point in dwelling on that point as it had not happened. But it was disturbing to think that if she developed cancer that she might not move forward from a position of high hope.

Thus, I had a bit different reaction, than one might expect, when in 2007, as a result of a routine mammogram, I was called back to the radiologist's office for an MRI and ultrasound. It was the Women's Radiology Center, headed by Susan Curry, M.D., in Orlando, that made a diagnosis that I had an early stage, but aggressive breast cancer.

I would later observe that when I went for my mammogram that they had a cute practice of giving one a little teddy bear to hold during the mammogram. They took it back when the test was over. When they had me back for the MRI and ultrasound, they gave me the teddy bear and did not take it back. One did not want to receive a permanent gift of the teddy bear. Nonetheless, my reaction to the diagnosis was not one of despair or fear but, rather, I was glad that my cousins were not facing that diagnosis, after having gone through so much pain with their mothers.

Christian's illness and death in 2000 also had a profound effect on my reaction. First, Christian had shown so much bravery and had gone through so much before his death, that I could not imagine that anything I would face would remotely compare to the suffering that he had endured during his seven years of illness. Second, through grace and faith, I had experienced the healing comfort of the Lord and I was in a place of absolute faith that Christian was in the Lord's hands. I had complete faith as I faced the next period of weeks and months, that God's healing grace was with me, and that no matter what, I would be healed, either here or with the Lord and my beloved Christian in heaven. I felt little fear.

Because of my family history, I decided that I would go to Mayo Clinic in Jacksonville, for a determination of the best course of action following my diagnosis.

The first diagnosis was that I was in the earliest stage of breast cancer. I approached my first appointment with optimism. However, I had gone online by the time of my appointment and realized that the form of cancer created an intrinsic risk of metastasis. I had a long list of questions as I went through an entire day of tests and analysis. Mayo was as impressive as I had thought it would be. And two factors stood out to me. By the time that I got to each appointment, the doctor had the notes and analysis from the previous doctor available to him or her. The diagnosis and suggested treatment would be the result of a coordinated team approach.

By the end of the day, the team explained my options and their recommendations in detail, answering my many questions. They had run my test results and history through two different national databases tied into the National Cancer Institute. The results were clear. With a lumpectomy and five years of chemotherapy, the prognosis was that I would have a 70% chance of recurrence. With a double mastectomy, I had less than a 2% chance of recurrence. Less than the general population for cancer. A no-brainer.

It was time to have at it. The date was set. I let my family know and my dear sister, Nancy, and Will, planned to be present and set up their schedules so that one or the other of them would be with me in the month following my surgery.

My initial surgery went as well as could be expected. I had a simultaneous reconstruction which left me with a natural appearance but meant a ten-hour surgery. A lengthy surgery is a challenge for both the physicians and the patient. It was not a piece of cake and the days and weeks would be challenging. The first indication, however, that the recommendation and my decision, had been on the mark, came when the pathology report returned showing that I already had developed cancer cells in both breasts. Thankfully, there was no indication of any involvement of any lymph nodes.

There were other challenges. I was among the small percentage of patients who have difficulty with their wounds. I had to have several surgeries, and extra steps would have to be taken to assist in healing my incisions. My original surgery was in September 2007. I would later go back in 2008 and 2014, for complete recovery. After eight years, there has never been any indication of a recurrence of the cancer.

I have never forgotten, for one moment, the price paid by my grandmother and my aunts. Their journeys contributed to the body of knowledge which developed in the intervening years before I was diagnosed. And not only did Christian's example of courage throughout his illness remain at the forefront of my thoughts. So too the courage of my grandmother and my aunts were a part of my thoughts and prayers.

My surgeon, Dr. Galen Perdikis, was there for me in every way. During the period when my incision was not properly healing, there was considerable concern about potential outcomes. I had a visiting nurse daily for six weeks who changed dressings and helped with other treatments prescribed by Dr. Perdikis. Both Dr. Perdikis, and my primary physician, gave me their cell phone numbers, with instructions, that if I observed any adverse change whatsoever, that I was to call one or the other of them. I wound up sleeping sitting up on my couch for about three months before I felt comfortable enough to sleep in my bed. While there were some complications, I am a grateful and hopeful survivor of breast cancer.

My family and friends were there for me. And totally supportive. And at each moment, I knew, no matter what, that I am always in the healing hands of the Lord.

CHAPTER 24

Do Not Become Your Enemy

———◆———

"You have heard that it was said, 'Love your neighbor
and hate your enemy.   But I tell you, love your
enemies and pray for those who persecute you, that
you may be children of your Father in heaven."

MATTHEW 5:43-48

In 2010, WILL, MY OLDER son, stopped with two friends at a favorite down-town restaurant in Wilmington, N.C., for a slice of pizza, before heading home.   It was after 1:00 a.m.

While the restaurant had a bar and was a favorite of locals, it was not known as being particularly rowdy, even late at night.

As Will stood with his friends, a bottle was thrown by someone at the door, and almost hit a young woman, sitting at a nearby table.   Will looked briefly at the door and then asked the young lady whether a man standing at the door had just thrown the bottle at her.   A server standing next to the table spoke up and said, "No, I think he was trying to hit me. He complained that I had not served him quickly enough."

Will glanced back over his shoulder and then turned back to eat his pizza and continue a discussion with his friends.   One of the men was moving to

149

Colorado. The evening had been a send-off party for him. He was an Army veteran who had been wounded in Iraq and walked with a cane. The guys soon finished their pizza and drinks and walked towards the door to leave.

Will would comment later that it registered on him, in the brief moment that he had glanced at the man at the door, that the man appeared angry. So as Will and his friends were leaving, Will said he diverted his eyes away from the man who was now facing a table by the door.

Will's friend who walked with a cane was the first out of the door. Will followed. Just as he started to exit, Will heard something behind him. He turned to see that the friend behind him was bleeding. He had been hit over the head with a bottle. Will called to his other friend, who, by this time had crossed the street, and turned back to assist his friend who had just been hurt.

The next thing Will knew was that he was in a hospital. When he turned back towards the door of the restaurant, the man who had thrown the bottle, took a glass and smashed Will directly in the face with it. Will fell backward on the sidewalk, hitting the curb and cracking the back of his head open. His face had multiple broken bones.

About the time that Will regained consciousness in the hospital, I received a call, in NY, from one of Will's friends who had been at the scene. He explained what had happened. He went on to explain that Will had had so much blood going down his throat from the initial assault that he had stopped breathing on the spot. While the police and medics had been called—Will was not breathing.

Will had a guardian angel that night. A marine medic was walking past the scene and realized that Will, who was covered in blood, was not breathing. He cleared Will's throat and got him to a sitting position, still unconscious, so that he could breathe.

Will would be unconscious for almost an hour.

Will called me shortly after he gained consciousness. I packed and left by 4:00 a.m. to drive to NC. It was faster for me to drive than it would have been to catch a plane.

When I arrived at the hospital, the doctor described to me that Will's face looked like a cracked eggshell. There were so many breaks in the bones that they could not count them all. Doctors had stitched the back of Will's head, but there was little else at that point for them to do. Will's nose was so badly broken that it could not even be set.

It would be a year to the week that Will would have reconstructive surgery on his face. Doctors explained that the swelling in Will's face would have to recede totally. It would be months before they could operate. They also wanted to allow as many bones as possible to heal on their own. Will would be in pain for many months and develop breathing problems because of the assault on his face. Thankfully, he did not suffer a brain injury from his fall onto the sidewalk.

Will had never seen or spoken to the man who attacked him before that night. He was in his early twenties, the son of a wealthy business person, and known to police as a troublemaker. He had been in fights before but had not been arrested. As in other cases that the public has seen, where a wealthy parent was involved, the man was insulated from any legal recourse on Will's part. Will missed weeks of work time and endured pain for a year. All parts of his life were affected. There would be little financial recovery from the man, who without any provocation whatsoever, had inflicted so much pain.

The man was arrested on the spot and in the following days charged with aggravated assault, inflicting serious injury. The charge carried a five-year mandatory prison sentence. Police told me that they were considering an attempted murder charge but ultimately decided that the situation would not rise to that level. I hoped that the man would serve all five years.

Months would pass, and Will would get reports from time to time from the victim liaison. There would come a day that he would get a message from the district attorney.

The man was going to plead guilty to a lesser charge and would be put on probation. He would also be required to complete an anger management course. He would have to pay some of Will's medical costs and for some of the time Will had missed at work. There would be no payment for Will's pain and suffering. Or for his business which had been drastically affected.

Will had an astounding response to the news that this young man would walk free after doing so much damage. "I am glad he is not going to prison," he said. "If he goes to prison he will just come out with more hatred. And he will be likely to hurt or kill someone in the future." Will was willing to forgive, as we are all asked to forgive, in the Lord's prayer.

Will Wagner

Will reminded me of my comments in the past that hatred breeds hatred.

In the face of a scary world, where so much tragedy is brought about by what appears to be a total loss, at times, of humanity, I can't help but think of the Ten Commandments. From the earliest days of civilization, we have been given God's guidance, which we have ignored or not been able to heed. Thus, when, we as humanity, committed unspeakable sins, through faith, Christ paid the price for our sins. And continues to do so today.

Christ brought us forgiveness.

In fear of weakness and victimization, hopefully, we will not become as a country, along with other countries throughout the world, the enemy we despise. Hopefully, we will show strength, while recognizing that acting out of fear and hatred, will also lead us down perilous paths.

While I experienced anger towards the man who so viciously attacked Will, I did not feel hatred. And later, I was grateful for the example of forgiveness that Will provided. Hopefully, this man will recognize the second chance that he was given. And appreciate the significance. I do not suggest that those who commit crimes should not be held accountable. However, from the point of view of healing, where Will was concerned, I was grateful that as Will journeyed through the challenge of healing, that he had not turned to hatred for solace.

CHAPTER 25
A Knock at the Door

———◆———

WHEN PEOPLE ASK ME HOW I got to New Smyrna Beach, Florida, I always answer, "God brought me here." I have heard others say the same thing. It is a wonderful and caring community. Living in New Smyrna Beach had not been on the horizon in 1999.

It was in the months following Christian's death, while still living with my brother at my parents' home, that I discovered New Smyrna Beach, directly east of Orlando. It would turn out that much of my therapy over the past fifteen years has been to walk on the wonderful sandy beaches of New Smyrna. I now live a mile from the ocean on the intracoastal waterway.

The blessings of a community were brought home to me by a wonderful friend, Christa Kelsey. I met Christa in 2001 and instantly appreciated her smile that brought light to the whole town, and her caring ways. Over the two years after Christian's death, several of my oldest friends, including Carol, whom I have written about, either died suddenly or from cancer. Christa knew this and called me years ago to invite me to join her and a group of friends for dinner. It was a group of friends, some of whom had known each other from childhood, who had dinner together every Tuesday night. There have been few Tuesday nights that I have missed in the intervening years if I am in town.

These friends became family. They say that family should treat each other as friends. And that friends should treat each other as family. We have supported each other, at times become irritated with each other, cared for each other, and loved each other. I cannot imagine the past fourteen years without these friends.

There came a day when some well-wishers from the Tuesday night group would say to me, "Susan, you have to get out more. No one is going to come knocking at your door." They encouraged me in the healing process to open my heart to the possibility of a loving relationship. I knew that the day might come when I might be ready for that. But I was in no hurry.

In 2008, I had been living in my condo for seven years and had become the association president. Another individual had served for seven years and eventually had resigned from what is somewhat a thankless effort. I had been named the president by default. No one else in the building would accept the 'opportunity'.

As such, I had keys to all of the condos so that maintenance, response to emergencies, and other assistance could be facilitated.

In 2007, we had a seasonal renter, whose first name was Bob, who had eventually been asked to vacate his temporary condo, for too much partying. He was well past the age of a mid-life crisis. While some might appreciate his zest for life, his late night celebrations were not appreciated by his neighbors. Upon his departure, there was agreement in the building that he would not be welcomed back.

I was a bit chagrined the following year to hear messages on my phone, from Bob, asking that I provide him the telephone number of one of the people who did not want him back in the building. Bob had heard that she was doing a seasonal rental and wanted to contact her. I was traveling and decided to put the messages aside until I could speak with the owner whose number he was requesting.

One day there was a knock at my door. It was a maintenance worker asking if I could let him into the same owner's condo upstairs to check a leak on the balcony. I knew that she was in Georgia, so I said yes that I would accompany him to the condo. I took the keys, knocked on the door to be sure that she was not there, and let the two of us into the condo. The maintenance worker took only a couple of minutes to see what he had come to inspect, and we left. Being responsible, I, of course, locked the door when we left.

About an hour later there was a knock at my front door. There stood a stranger. He said, "Hi, my name is Bob Carter, I have just moved in upstairs. I think someone was in my condo." It was not the Bob who had lived in our building the previous season. He was, I now realized, a different Bob who had tried to call me for information about the owner upstairs. Since I had not returned his calls, he had found another way to locate the owner, and rent the condo.

I quickly answered that I had been the one in his new condo with the maintenance worker.

"Well, he said. You locked me out." He had walked to the store, leaving the door unlocked and his keys on the counter.

I quickly apologized and got the keys to let him into his own condo.

Bob was polite, but I could see that he was irritated. I guessed that he also remembered that I was the one who had not returned his phone calls. Shortly after that, I called him to see if I might buy him a glass of wine at a favorite spot on the water to make amends.

Seven years later, on September 21, 2014, Bob and I were married by my brother-in-law, the Reverend John Loving, in Central Park, in N.Y.

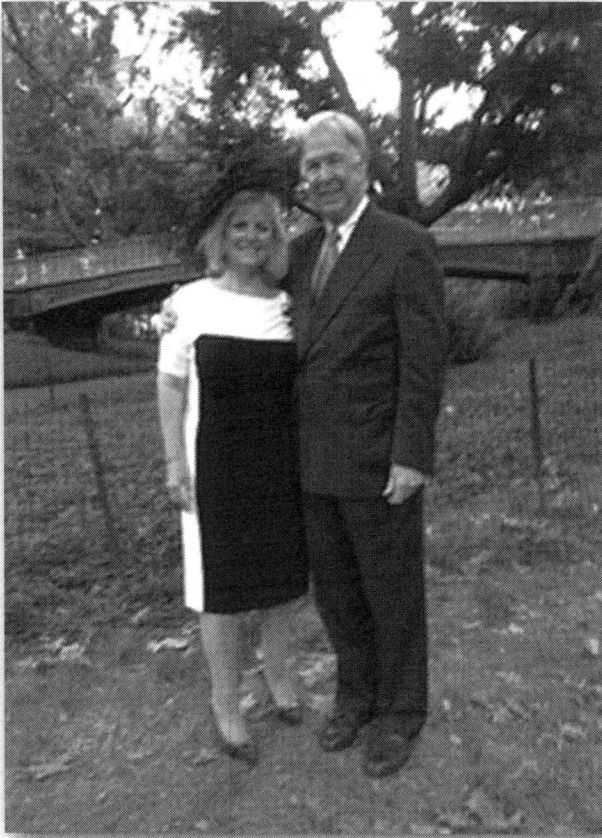

Susan and Bob on Their Wedding Day 2014

We traveled quite a path to that day in Central Park. My locking Bob out of his condo might have been an indicator to him of what lay ahead. However, first, by forgiveness, then by Bob's willingness to travel the bumps ahead, God brought a wonderful, loving, caring man to my front door. A person who would ultimately want to share life, hand in hand, in faith. And some splendid adventures. I had failed to answer Bob's calls and had decided before I met him that he did not belong in our building.

And yet, God found a way to open the door to my heart and to let me love deeply again.

There is no question, that at times in life, there have been knocks at the door, that perhaps I did not answer. Times when the Lord might have sent someone to my door whom I might have assisted or served in some other way. I try not to spend time in regret. I try not to ask, 'why', as it relates to Christian. God reveals answers in His way. The only real answer that I found was that the way forward, was the assurance of the Lord's love, for both of my children, my family, and my friends. And for my enemies. He loves me not for the good that I do but for the good that He does.

He does not love my enemies less for what they do but because He is love. I now listen for those knocks at the door. And pray, that always, they will be God's love showing me the way.

CHAPTER 26
Triumph of His Love

"For where two or three gather in my
name, there am I with them."

MATHEW 18:20

IN 2000, IT SEEMED THAT I had lost almost everything that had value to me. I had lost my beloved Christian and both of my parents, and less significant, my business. There were not many minutes or even moments without pain.

At the same time, in God's hands, I had everything to go forward. I had faith that Christian was with the Lord. Soon I realized that for Will to have any hope for healing, that I had to heal. It would be missing the mark, entirely, to ignore the wonderful gift of Will's life, by burying myself in my grief. It would be a double tragedy for this young man not to have the opportunity to feel fully loved and to use his wonderful gifts as the Lord intends.

A loving family and friends reached out to me to provide support. And I had gifts for the soul.

A few short weeks after Christian's death I was with my friend, Carol, for the morning. She had asked me to go with her to a home where she was painting a massive mural. Once there, I needed a few minutes to myself and asked if I might take her car to get myself a cup of coffee.

As I pulled once again into a McDonald's and turned off the motor to her car, I cried out loud, "Christian, if you could just let me know that you are all right."

I went directly to the lady's room to splash some water on my face and to try to pull myself together. I then got in line to get myself a drink. As I stood there, a man who had been sitting in a booth stepped up to me. He asked if I was all right. I answered, "No not really. I lost my son several weeks ago, and I am not doing a good job keeping myself together today."

With that, he answered me, "I am an architect. I have never had any experience like this ever. Or done something like this. But God told me to tell you that your son is fine."

I told him of the words said aloud in my car. I had never seen this man before, and I would never see him again. At that moment, we both knew that the Holy Spirit had moved through him to deliver this important and almost lifesaving message to me. He had instantly become a prophet—a speaker of the truth. How grateful I am to the Lord. And how grateful I am that this man had the courage and faithfulness to deliver this gift for the soul. He did not hesitate when he heard that still small voice. Without embarrassment or second thought, the two of us sat down in the booth in McDonald's and prayed. This was one of a number of occurrences that let me know that the presence of the Lord was with me. And more importantly, that Christian is with Him. The Lord is our shepherd.

For many years now I have asked God for daily guidance in my life. There have continued to be challenges, and certainly at times heartache. In 2007, there was the diagnosis of breast cancer and a double mastectomy. In 2010, the unbearable almost occurred when Will was nearly killed while walking out of a restaurant. Both of these events entailed lengthy periods of physical and emotional healing.

In the midst of the journey, however, there have also been many days of joy, wonder, satisfaction and opportunities to love and to serve.

This book began as a solitary endeavor. As grieving, in many ways, is personal, so too is writing. However, God shines his light of good through the body of Christ. God's action is always intended for the good of the whole. As the story and the message unfolded, I realized that the Lord had brought me to a path on which to seek direction and to witness to the gift of God's unfolding mystery. I became increasingly aware of an urgency to focus not only on what I was writing, or my personal grief, but on the questions and answers that my writing generated. Some were not questions that I could, or that I felt that God wanted me, to answer on my own.

In my expanded family there have been differences and blessing to be understood. We have continued to discover within our new family, that we all have a deep commitment to the Lord. We come to that understanding, at times, from different vantage points. In listening to each other, we know that through each other, we hear and learn God's word.

A long friendship with Lois Jordan, who is truly faithful and dedicated to the Lord, led to a Bible study with what would become a close group of other faithful women. Again, while dedicated, we soon discovered that our diverse backgrounds, and the way that the Lord has unfolded to each of us on this journey called life, surfaced even deeper questions to be discussed, and positions to be understood and expanded rather than defended.

Each of the women in the Bible study is on a challenging journey. During our studies, we were all given a real gift in the form of a trilogy, "The Christian Life Trilogy", written by Reverend Charlie Holt. The combination of the study of the Word, the accompanying study guide and video for the trilogy, and our personal and lively discussions, seemed to illuminate for each one of us, where we needed to focus. Each of the books served as a guide and a call, to contemplate the price Christ paid for us, on how we are called to follow in faith and change for Him, and how we all are moved by the Holy Spirit to carry God's love to others.

For me, it was a call to urgency and accountability, and almost as one does with the final steps of a Rubik's cube, to click into place the pieces and answers that were still floating in my head. There were no longer any excuses to delay completing what I had started.

Our group had the gift of attending and worshiping, at St. Peter's Episcopal Church, in Lake Mary, Fl., on Pentecost Sunday, 2016, to hear Reverend Holt's message and guidance from the Lord. Reverend Holt's answer to the call of ministry has allowed God to speak through him. It was clear that he reaches out to understand the journeys of his congregation as well as visitors to the church. We each felt welcomed personally.

I had just begun to surface my manuscript to seek critical input from trusted friends and guides. Ultimately, the purpose of any ministry is to join others to move deeper in our faith, and to make a difference in our world. We are called to do this together in the church—meaning as part of the body of Christ. As we met Reverend Holt, I was exactly at the point where I needed confirmation, that my intended purpose in writing this book, namely to bear worthy witness to the Lord's amazing love through-out my life, and to provide ministry to those who may walk similar paths has been served. I feel truly blessed that Reverend Holt then allowed me to seek his counsel as I entered the final phases of completing "Loved Through The Pain." While writing about my personal journey began as a solitary endeavor, it became evident, that it was through the involvement of the body of Christ, that it would be transformed.

Proverbs 3:5-6 "Don't put your confidence in your own un-derstanding. In all your ways acknowledge him, and he will direct your path."

While I have described my personal journey with the Lord, and so greatly appreciate the love and care given by so many who have enriched my life, the real message is in understanding the difference between love devel-oped through our relationships and the unconditional love of God.

Romans 5:8 "But God demonstrates his own love for us in this: While we were still sinners, Christ died for us."

We are called to love our neighbors as ourselves. We are called to love our enemies. And we are called to understand God's love for us.

Christ surrendered himself on the cross out of love for all of us. It was the fool hearty who called out for him to save himself. And it is in fool-ishness that we attempt to live our lives as though we can do it ourselves.

Through faith, love, and prayer, we each can hear that still small voice, glorify his Name, and bring a bit of heaven to earth. It can be an extraor-dinary moment to realize that as minute as each of us is in the universe, each of us has more atoms than the stars we see in the sky, and the Lord infuses and cares for every atom of our being. Through His love, we are part of His glory.

1 Peter 1:8 "Though you have not seen him, you love him; and even though you do not see him now, you believe in him and are filled with an inexpressible and glorious joy, for you are receiving the end result of your faith, the salvation of your souls."

Acknowledgements

———

As described throughout this book, I have been blessed by a lifetime of love, forgiveness and support of my family. To Will, Nancy, John, Rob, Dawn and cousins Janie and Anne, thank you for always being there. For my other cousins, thank you for a lifetime of fun and love. For my nephews, Ward and Brad, I give thanks for their awesome lives and for their care for Will, Christian and for me.

I give special thanks to my husband, Bob, who has supported me through many ups and downs, and through the hours, weeks and months of processing, writing and editing. Every day is enriched by his faith, love, loyalty, laughter and and inner strength.

I have been blessed with my blended family. I give thanks for Jeff and Robbie, Tom and Lisa, and Lori and Kevin who also have become my sons and daughters. I give special thanks to my mother-in-law, Joyce Walsh, 94. She is one spunky lady and has been a dear friend. A nod to Pat, my sister-in law, for her caring ways.

In the Carter family in 2013, beloved Roberta (Robbie) Mary Spensieri, at age 56, went to be with the Lord. It was a blessing and an honor to know her. Robbie had had a massive stroke at the age of twenty-nine which left her a paraplegic for twenty-seven years. She was not able to speak aloud, but her eyes, her heart, and her spirit spoke volumes. She was able, through her companions and technology to convey her thoughts and love. She had a wonderful sense of humor. She used her humor to speak truths. Her bravery and Jeff's devotion have been beacons for hundreds in their hometown of Saratoga Springs, NY. On the day of her funeral, the service had to be delayed, as hundreds of people turned out to pay their respect to her and her family. That included many from the Saratoga Springs fire department. And a Mayor and ex-Mayor. Once again we've all called upon the Lord for healing, particularly for Jeff and for her parents. All in the family know that she is in the Lord's hands.

So too, in joining this family, I became a grandmother. It has been great fun to see Steve, Bekah, Leah and Caleb grow into young adults setting off on journeys of their own. I got to know the thrill of being called "Grandma" when Bob and I stepped off a plane in California, and Moriah and Sierrah rushed up to greet me. Their brothers, Zack and Carter, were equally welcoming. All of these young people walk in faith and are beautiful reflections of the Lord's presence and the faith of their parents and grandparents.

For my wonderful friends and prayer partners in Bible study. We all remind ourselves and each other to come back to the Word—the Bible. And that we are brought along these paths, not for our personal satisfaction, but rather that we may witness, serve, and join in the whole church of Christ. We all have had WOW moments during our studies and gatherings. And so we dubbed ourselves, WOW, meaning, "Women of the Word".

Each week through our studies, we have taken time for reflection and prayer. We have brought alerts and prayers for others who have come to our attention. Together, we have witnessed God's faithfulness, week after week, as we have seen prayers answered in ways that we had not imagined.

These women helped transform my focus in writing, from a solo endeavor to a witness and ministry for others through their mutual care, prayer, insight, and commitment to studying the Word together. I give thanks for Hope Schmitt, Suzanne Jarrell, Sherrie Cunningham, Julie Rambo, Teresa Beasley and Lisa Dunphy for their faith and faithfulness to our studies and our friendships. And a special word of thanks to Lois Jordan, for her faith and many years of friendship.

As in so many other times and ways, I feel God has directed the path of this book. I am grateful to Lois, Mary Gerlach, and Linda Fay, who read and made valuable observations and suggestions on my early manuscript. I give thanks to God that my sisters and I were led to the writing and guidance of Reverend Holt. And I give special thanks to him as well. He has not hesitated to bring his faith, wisdom, ministry and prayer to assist me.

———◆———

National Suicide Prevention Lifeline
Call 1-800-273-8255
1-800-273-TALK
http://www.suicidepreventionlifeline.org

Holy Bible
New International Version
Scripture Quotations

Hebrews 12:1 " Let us through everything that hinders page 1
Romans 8:28 "And we know that in all page 4
John 10:10 "The thief comes only to steal and kill and destroy page 25
Psalm 121:1-8 "I lift up my eyes to the mountains—where does my help come from? Page 34
Mathew 7:7 "Ask, and it will be given to you –page 41
Psalm 8 1:2 "Lord, our Lord, how majestic is your name page 45
Mathew 19:14 "Jesus said, 'Let the little children come to me page 46
Colossians 1:9-10 "We continually ask God to fill you with the knowledge of his will page 46
Mathew 29:36 "Love your neighbor as yourself." Page 52
Ephesians 4:32 "Be kind and compassionate to one another Page 71
Mathew 6:24 "No one can serve two masters." Page 85
James 1:17 "Every good and perfect gift is from above…" Page 98
Job 11:13015 "Surrender your heart to God, turn to him in prayer Page 125
John 3:16 "For God so loved the world,   Page 161
Isaiah 53:12 "He bore the sins of many Page 161
Psalm 34:18 "The Lord is near to the brokenhearted Page 162
Psalm 50:15 "Call upon Me in the day of trouble;   Page 171
1 Peter 4:18 "Each one should use whatever gift he has Page 189
Job 34:12 "It is unthinkable that God would do wrong, that the Almighty would pervert justice." Page 198
Matthew 25:35-40 "For I was hungry and you gave me food,   Page 202
Philippians 1:3 "I thank God every time I remember you." Page 203
Mathew 5:43 "You have heard that it was said,   Page212
Mathew 18:20 "For where two or three gather in my name, there am I with them." Page 225

Proverbs 3:5-6 "Don't put your confidence in your own understanding. Page 230

Romans 5:8 "But God demonstrates his own love for us Page 230

1 Peter 1:8 "Though you have not seen him, you love him; and even though you do not see him now Page 231

About the Author

SUSAN WAGNER CARTER SHARES IN the spirit of the living God. She has walked the paths of writer, mother, world traveler, inventor, entrepreneur, and former sub-cabinet government executive. She is a native Floridian. Her father was a newspaper man and eventually moved the family to New York. The family's move led to Susan living all over the world, and in cities across the United States. She returned to central Florida sixteen years ago.

Susan was married to a US diplomat and served in embassies in the Congo, Guinea, and Morocco. During the years in Africa, Susan wrote for US and foreign newspapers and magazines, including Fortune and The Miami Herald. During those demanding years, the Word of the Lord, prayer, and meditation led to a lifelong journey in the Spirit. Her deepened faith, and God's comfort and love, sustained her through the loss of her younger son, Christian, in April 2000.

In Washington, D.C., Susan served as Legislative Assistant to US Congressman John Dellenback and in White House and related positions under Presidents Ford, Carter, and Reagan. She served as Special Assistant to the US Comptroller of the Currency and as Executive Director of the Commodity Futures Trading Commission. She left the government to design and patent the first entirely computerized futures trading exchange system, adopted by commodity exchanges in the US and abroad. She then answered a call to serve as Vice President of Finance of World Vision International, a humanitarian relief organization.

In recent years, she has worked behind the scenes, with her older son, Will, who has developed breakthrough high definition technology.

Susan's journey in the Spirit has led her to answer calls for prayer, service, and leadership. This book is her personal witness to God's love, her understanding of the sacrifice made for all of us, and how faith changed her life. May it be a beacon for others whom it may touch.

34100628R00102

Made in the USA
Columbia, SC
12 November 2018